CW00836128

Grow Your Own Carrot

Grow Your Own Carrot

Stop struggling and
start succeeding

Bob Griffiths and Chris Kaday

HELP YOURSELF

Copyright © 2004 by Bob Griffiths and Chris Kaday

First published in Great Britain in 2004

The right of Bob Griffiths and Chris Kaday to be identified
as the Authors of the Work has been asserted by them in accordance
with the Copyright, Designs and Patents Act 1988.

10 9 8 7 6 5 4 3 2 1

British Library Cataloguing in Publication Data
A record for this book is available from the British Library

ISBN 0 340 86285 8

Typeset in ACaslonRegular by Avon DataSet Ltd,
Bidford-on-Avon, Warwickshire

Printed and bound in Great Britain by
Bookmarque Ltd, Croydon, Surrey

The paper and board used in this paperback are natural recyclable products
made from wood grown in sustainable forests. The manufacturing processes
conform to the environmental regulations of the country of origin.

Hodder & Stoughton
A Division of Hodder Headline Ltd
338 Euston Road
London NW1 3BH
www.madaboutbooks.com

We would like to thank all those who took part in the Test Team for their efforts and commitment to the process. You inspired us to create this book.

Contents

Acknowledgements

I would like to thank my partner Chris, whose love, patience and understanding helped me turn my book writing Goal into published Reality. Your inspiration made Obstacles evaporate and Options appear – thank you.

Chris

I would like to thank my wife Sam and son Eliot for just being wonderful, and Franziska and Patrick for giving so much support during the hard times. I would also acknowledge Coachmaster, the coaching software I developed which gave me the idea for the book in the first place.

Bob

Introduction

This is a book about change. It is designed to help you to achieve whatever you want in any area of your life. The writers' aim is not only to arouse your interest but to galvanise you into action. We will help you decide on a Goal, and then lead you step by step through a powerful process that will get you there. All you have to do is follow each step with care and consideration. It sounds simple, doesn't it? But we recognise that, for the great majority of people, making change is not that easy. If it were, we would all be taking control of our lives and changing all the time. Together we will explore why we struggle to make the changes we need to achieve our Goals. Then we will show you how the path to success can be made relatively simple and straightforward.

So why the carrot?

We have called this book *Grow Your Own Carrot* for some very good reasons. We all know about using the stick and the carrot to thrash or tempt a donkey to move forward. Sometimes we all need a proverbial stick to make a shift, but there is little to

1

be gained by continually beating ourselves up. Sweet juicy carrots are a far more attractive incentive.

Motivational carrots come in various shapes and sizes and they can be offered to us in numerous ways. While our motivation sometimes comes from the outside, there is no doubt that the best carrots are those you grow yourself. When you are not dependent on others to provide your motivation, you are capable of achieving almost anything.

So, you might well ask, how can you grow these wonderful carrots? Enter the GROW process, which will give you a simple step-by-step method for achieving almost any Goal within your control and capacity. As you will see as you read through this book, the GROW process will provide you with a framework to stop struggling and start succeeding.

What is the GROW process?

The GROW process has been used by life coaches, counsellors and consultants for over twenty years to bring about lasting change in their clients. We believe it is the best-structured methodology available for achieving Goals, making decisions and solving problems. It works by guiding you to consider your issues in an organised way and to develop your own solutions, rather than be told by others how you should think and act. When you have chosen your own Goals and how you will achieve them it is far more likely that you will achieve your desired outcome. You can read more about GROW in Appendix 2.

The acronym GROW stands for Goal, Reality, Obstacles, Options and Way Forward. (So technically it should be called 'GROOW' but we didn't think that sounded so neat!)

We will introduce the stages briefly now, and then in subsequent chapters we will give more details about each stage, together with exercises and questions to help you work on your own Goal. At the beginning of the book we include a section called 'GROW express' which you can use as a quick reference guide to see all the process in one place. If you are impatient to start or you want to skip a particular chapter, you will find the essence of each stage of the GROW process with Reading Hints and key questions.

The stages of GROW

Here is an overview of the stages of the GROW process. You will find much more detail about each stage in the relevant chapters.

G the Goal

This is the end point, where you want to be. The Goal should be defined in such a way that it is very clear to you when you have achieved it.

R the Reality

This is how far you are away from your Goal. If you were to look at all the steps you need to take in order to achieve your Goal, your Reality would be the number of those steps you have completed so far.

O the Obstacles

There are Obstacles stopping you getting from where you are now to where you want to go. If there were no Obstacles you would already have reached your Goal.

O the Options

Once Obstacles have been identified you need to find ways of dealing with them if you are to make progress. We call these your Options.

W is for Way Forward

The Options then need to be converted into action steps which will take you to your Goal. We call these the Way Forward.

An example of using the GROW process to achieve a Goal

Imagine that you want to achieve a health Goal. For instance: 'To bring my weight down to 120 pounds in three months and keep it down'.

That is your **Goal**. The GROW approach would then be to establish your **Reality** by stating what your weight is now. You would then ask yourself awareness questions to deepen your understanding of what is happening when you try to lose weight, thus identifying your **Obstacles**. These questions could include:

- When I have been able to lose weight – what made the difference?
- What is the difference between the times I am able to keep weight off and the times when I put it on again?
- Am I sure I know the best way to lose weight?

If you genuinely answer these questions you will discover new information about what works and does not work for you in terms of weight loss, and create some potential for change. It then becomes possible to create some strategies or **Options** which get around the **Obstacles**. These could include looking at which diets or exercise regimes work best for you, or finding a specific type of support for yourself. Once you know the strategies that are likely to work you can establish a **Way Forward** which involves taking action steps. This is where you commit to what you will do in the short term to put the strategies into effect. For instance, one action might be asking a particular person for support, and another might be to buy a different selection of foods.

In this weight loss example we have quickly worked through each stage of the GROW process, using questions to look at the issues in a focused way to the point where you would feel able to move forward, by yourself.

Without the GROW process most people have an inner dialogue which goes something like this:

I want to lose weight, I feel fat and unattractive. But I have no self-discipline, I like sweet things too much, I have never been able to keep weight off. My wife keeps telling me to lose weight and I don't like being nagged.

The desire to lose weight ends up fighting with your desire to hold on to the status quo, and you keep going around in circles and find it difficult to move forward. We will explore this cycle more in Chapter 8 on Obstacles. The GROW process gives you a sure-fire route to breaking that vicious circle and moving towards your Goal.

As you work through this book you will find a series of questions relating to each stage of the GROW process which are designed to help you work through your own issues and challenges. As we have already said, this book is for action, not for interest alone, so it is important that you set yourself a clear Goal that you want to achieve in your own life as you continue to read. We will also help you do this.

Trust the process

GROW is a process, and as such each stage has to be thoroughly worked through before continuing to the next. The quality of the work you put in at one stage will directly impact the quality of the result you achieve in the next. For example, if you do not identify as many Obstacles as possible that stand in the way of you achieving your Goal, your Options for moving forward will be similarly limited. We have also found that the GROW process works in both directions. For example, digging deep to understand your Reality could well lead you to revise your original Goal.

As you work through this book we hope there will be times of revelation and celebration as you gain confidence, move forward and achieve your Goals. It is also possible, or even likely, that there will be times of confusion and frustration, coupled with a strong desire to put this book down as it seems to be too great an effort. All we can suggest is that you trust the process.

Throughout this book you will find many exercises designed to test your resolve, stimulate your thinking and open up many possibilities. The *ASK YOURSELF* question at the end of this introduction is typical of these. The more candidly you work through the exercises, the greater the insights you will gain along the way.

Once you have proved that the GROW process works for you, we will show you how to set and achieve Goals jointly with others. This could be with your life partner or with a group at work or in your social life. This takes the GROW process into entirely new territory where the challenges and gains are even greater. See Appendix 1, 'Using GROW for shared Goals', for more information.

Making the effort

But is it worth all the effort? Definitely! To prove it for yourself, think of a Goal you have achieved in the past. It could be making some change in your life, acquiring a new skill, travelling alone or something quite different. You might not have thought of it as a specific Goal at the time, but what matters is that you wanted to achieve something and you felt a real sense of satisfaction from the outcome. Cast your mind back to the exact point when you accomplished this Goal. See yourself there, hear any sounds which may have been around, feel again what it was like. There might even have been memorable tastes or smells connected to it. Take a moment to go there now and relive those moments.

The chances are you feel your energy rising, you might well feel lighter and brighter and maybe there is even a smile on your face. Yes, achieving Goals is an exhilarating feeling. As Chris's son Stefan exclaimed as they walked across the gang-plank to the beautiful white boat that had been their dream purchase for over a year: 'Yes! Yes! Yes!' While we delight in completing Goals at the time, they also stay in our memory and, as you have just experienced, can be recalled many years later. Achieving Goals feels good and has a positive impact on our lives. By learning how to stop struggling and start succeeding, you can achieve them more often.

Maintaining motivation

Our aim in writing this book is to help you bring change to any area of your life that you choose. This could be an issue you would like to resolve, a decision you need to make, something you want to change or bring into your life.

In order to make a real difference to you we knew that we had to make this book different as well. We do not want this book to be abandoned on your bookshelf in mid-chapter or possibly not read at all. So we have included tools and techniques to help maintain your motivation.

Chris was reminded of the many French learning courses, tapes and CDs he has bought over the years, usually immediately before or after making a trip to France. His dream was to run a workshop or meditation session in French or to be chatting away to the locals in Toulouse or Paris. In his mind he saw them falling about at his witty Gallic jokes that were both fluent and funny. So why is he still stumbling over the most simple of sentences? Why do the mysteries of French grammar continue to baffle him? You know the feeling. Once back home the motivation for learning, so strong when he inserted Tape One into the cassette player, simply faded away.

We are not assuming that you will remain fully motivated as you read this book. In fact, if you are anything like us, we are assuming that your motivation will reduce as the initial impetus fades, the tasks become more demanding and other things naturally compete for your space and time.

We have included a special chapter on staying motivated which you can use if you are finding the going a bit tough and need a boost. There you will find some great ideas to get started again if you feel you have lost your momentum.

Interest or action

As coaches with many years' experience we know you will get the most out of GROW if you select a Goal to work through, so that as you go through the process you can experience how it works in practice, not just in theory.

You might well have acquired this book with a specific Goal in mind, and if this is the case you will find all the guidance you need to achieve it. If, on the other hand, you are interested in the GROW process and how it can be applied, there is no better way to discover this than actually creating a real Goal and experiencing the different stages for yourself.

ASK YOURSELF

Am I reading this book out of interest or to take action?

Of course, you can read a detective novel without ever wanting to live like any of the characters. But this is not a work of fiction, it is a book written to help change your life. To do this you not only have to be interested but need to be motivated to act, so it is best to get your intentions straight right from the start.

But can a book really help you change your life? Certainly, if the timing is right, your motivation is strong, there is a clear process to follow and you have good support along the way. We will be helping you with all these requirements and more. We have even proved the material you are about to read, with forty participants in the GROW Test Team. You can find out all about this exciting programme in the next chapter.

Finally, from both of us, a sincere 'thank you' for reading this book. You have given us an opportunity to help *you* change your life. We take this responsibility very seriously and we hope you will too. Our aim is to inspire, motivate, stimulate, grab and propel you forward. We want to keep you continually interested, engaged and, above all, in action. You will need to be open and trusting and, most important, to stay with the process. This is quite a challenge. Are we up for it? You bet we are! We hope you will join us. With our information and your intent we can make a real difference. So let's get started!

1

The GROW Test Team

When we started writing *Grow Your Own Carrot* we discussed how, as coaches and business mentors, we had used GROW in the past to achieve success in many different client situations. Naturally we wanted to share some of our experiences with you, but then we realised that it was possible to demonstrate the GROW process in a more powerful way. We decided to conduct a live experiment by applying the GROW process to a cross-section of the European population at the same time as writing this book. Enter the GROW Test Team! From that moment writing this book became even more exciting and vibrant.

The objective of the Test Team project

Our objective in setting up the Test Team was to test the principles of this book in exactly the same way as you, the reader, would use them. We wanted to see how well the GROW process, when clearly explained, could help a random sample of people to achieve a wide variety of Goals. As well as supporting success we were also interested in understanding why people lost their way in the process and what we could do to keep them on track and engaged. By passing on this knowledge we realised we could increase the possibility that more readers like you would not only complete the book but, as the subtitle suggests, stop struggling and start succeeding. With the Test Team we were all going to learn together.

Recruiting the Test Team

Our first task was to select around forty participants from different European countries. They all wanted to achieve a Goal and were interested in the GROW process as a way of accomplishing it. We then facilitated a 'kick-off' workshop to set the scene by introducing everyone to each other and to the power of the GROW model. Having a whole group of people in the room all committed to making change in their lives was really thrilling. It felt like base camp at Everest, only better – without the cold or need for special gear!

We gave the Test Team eight weeks each to achieve a personal Goal of their own choice. We then followed them on their journey of change. The Test Team's experiences and insights are included in various sections of this book: how they viewed the setting of Goals, what had prevented them from achieving what they wanted in the past, the real changes they made and how these changes felt. They also shared what happened when things did not go as planned, how they overcame these difficulties and what they learned about themselves, their beliefs and behaviour when challenged by change.

To ensure the GROW process would have the maximum possibility of success we provided various ways of supporting and guiding our participants on their journey.

Building the support structures

Test Team participants were paired off into buddies with instructions that they should maintain regular contact and check in each week with at least a half-hour phone call or meeting. As we went through the GROW material our buddies connected for mutual support and worked together to expand the ideas and possibilities in the process. The buddies were also there for each other as a reference point and as support when one of them got stuck.

As one would expect, some buddy relationships never got off first base, while others turned into ongoing friendships which will probably endure for a lifetime. The buddy process proved to be a key part of the support structure, and that is why we recommend you create this for yourself as you go through the GROW process. Guidance for doing this is included in Chapter 4, 'Preparing the ground'.

A virtual community

We also set up a group on the web, where all the Test Team participants could post their insights and request and offer help. They also posted their Goals, Realities, Obstacles, Options and Ways Forward for all to see. The forum gave us somewhere to share the various issues which were common to the group. The web group was a real rallying point for the project, with well over 400 postings over the eight-week period. Some participants were regular contributors, while others went to the site for occasional inspiration and help.

Using email for support

We found that emailing was a great way to support personal progress. It required the person to clearly define their problem in print. We could then take time to read this and fully consider the problem and the possibilities. Our written reply could be read and re-read by the participant so they really understood our observations and suggestions.

Using teleclasses for learning

We held a one-hour teleclass every week throughout the programme to teach the various stages of the GROW process. A teleclass is like an ordinary class but conducted using a telephone conference call. In these sessions we discussed the particular issues raised by Test Team participants and everyone contributed to the solutions. In Chapter 4, 'Preparing the ground', we suggest a way for you to create this support community for yourself.

As someone said during a telephone session, 'It should be possible for anyone to achieve their Goal with all this support.' However, even with this intensive support only around half the original group of forty fully achieved their Goal. Bob, Chris and other participants spent a lot of time motivating some people to stay engaged with the process. There is a real lesson here. **All the support processes in the world will not achieve anything unless you are truly open and ready for change.** That is why you will find us inviting you throughout this book to do things differently and change those patterns.

The celebrations

We believe passionately in fun, joy and celebration. So eight weeks after our 'kick-off' events we held a party where we could acknowledge the achievements of our Test Team participants and all the hard work they had put in. You too could have your own celebration after achieving your first Goal with GROW. Maybe you can use GROW to plan the party as well. Think of the celebration as you read this book – all you have to do is get there, and we will help you every step of the way.

Some advice from our Test Team

A few months ago the Test Team were precisely where you are now, with no knowledge of the GROW process and no clear Goals. When the project was completed we asked them what advice they would give to someone starting on the journey. Here is a sample of their insights and experience:

> Even if the exercises seem a bit silly, do them. Try and get involved in using your imagination and your fun side. Try to think outside the box.
>
> Lindsey

> This process is easy to follow, straightforward, and can help you get the results you want. Your Obstacles will become your allies. What I like about the process is its practicality. I knew I was holding myself back and I didn't want a year and a half of therapy to find out what it was all about. With GROW you start with where you are now and grow forward.
>
> Matthew

> Be patient, go through every step of the process slowly and do not jump ahead. Be disciplined, stick to the process and slightly 'force' yourself to keep going if things are looking difficult. Seek advice if you get stuck, don't sit there and do nothing.
>
> Ray

> Don't do it alone – you may need some support. Be open-minded and flexible, be prepared to do things differently and don't lose your sense of humour. We are all good at

making excuses for ourselves, but this technique stops you doing just that. There is no magic, it just points out our own personal stumbling blocks that we will have been hitting over and over again and offers a chance to look at them differently.

Susan

Your best learning from this process will emerge from the part where you really get stuck. Don't give up, especially if that is when you normally get stuck.

Megan

You can do it! Life throws us curve balls along the way, challenges us, teaches us, moves us . . . if you stop trying and start listening, taking in, moving and doing whatever needs to be done, and follow the process, you will achieve your Goal.

Michelle

Make sure you choose a Goal you have difficulty achieving normally, something that's a real challenge and means questioning the way you think and behave. Elect to spend time with positive role models, not the moaners and groaners who will collude with any inaction on your part.

Marina

The GROW process has helped me to focus on my Goal, to identify my Obstacles and my Options. Within a relatively short time span of six weeks I achieved my Goal. Big sigh of relief!

Gabrielle

We hope this authentic feedback and the results obtained by the Test Team inspire and encourage you as much as they did us. Our thanks go out to them for the way they rose to the challenge and made a real difference through the application of this simple yet effective technique.

Notes

- All quotations in this book originate from the Test Team unless otherwise indicated.
- Substitute names for Test Team participants have been used throughout.
- We have used the masculine to refer to both genders.

2

GROW express:
the short cut to success

In this chapter you will find a 'quick reference' guide showing the entire GROW process in one place.

Below, you will find all the key points you need to use GROW for yourself or with someone else. We have included process, questions and hints. The right-hand column suggests pages you can refer to if you want more detail on a particular point.

Use 'GROW express' as follows:

1 Decide on the area of your life in which you want to set a Goal, and set a rough Goal.
2 Complete the section on preparation before you start.
3 Use the questions in the Goal section to turn your rough Goal into a clear and verifiable Goal statement.
4 Use the questions in the Reality section to produce a Reality statement showing how far you are away from the Goal.
5 Create your Obstacles statement, which will show what is stopping you progressing to your Goal.
6 Prepare your Option statement to demonstrate how you will get around the Obstacles.

7 Create your Way Forward action steps to take your Options forward.

8 Start putting the action steps into operation.

9 Use the Motivation section to maintain or recover your momentum.

10 Don't forget to celebrate at the end and along the way!

Stage definition	Process	Questions to consider	Hints	Chapter reference
Preparation	Consider what resources you need	Have I considered what resources I will need while I am working towards my Goal?		
	Create a positive environment	Have I prepared the physical environment which will support me?	Having an environment where you feel great gives you the best possible start	
	Set up a support club	Have I asked the individuals I want to be in my support club?	Improve your chances of success dramatically by building a support network and allowing preparation time	
		Have I set up my Goal folder?		
	Start keeping a journal	Have I considered why Goal setting has not worked for me in the past?	Learn from your experiences and you will not have to learn the same lessons again	

Stage definition	Process	Questions to consider	Hints	Chapter reference
G for Goal – your desired outcome the success criteria by which you know you have achieved your Goal	Create your Goal Statement	Am I clear on the type of Goal that want to achieve?	Understanding the type of Goal you want will help you plan effectively	Chapters 5 and 6
		Is the Goal in a SMART format? (Specific, Measurable, Achievable, Relevant, Time Phased)	The Goal should be something *you* really want, not something you think you should want	
	Test that it is clearly defined	Have I created a clear defining moment? Is there a sub Goal?	Know what you want to achieve and by when	
	Think through the implications of your Goal	Have I considered what I might lose or the risks inherent in achieving my Goal?	Gaining any Goal means letting go of something – be clear on what you might lose	
		Do I feel inspired by my Goal?	The best Goals are those that give you a big smile when you think about achieving them!	
		Have I used clear verbs to describe my Goal?	Verbs like 'identify' or 'develop' are less clear than verbs like 'buy' or 'enrol'	

Stage definition	Process	Questions to consider	Hints	Chapter reference
R for Reality How far you are from your Goal	Create a Reality statement that clearly shows where you are relative to the Goal	Is my Reality statement in the same terms as my Goal? What are the steps I need to complete to achieve my Goal? How many have I completed?	Don't confuse Reality with realistic. Describe the facts and avoid value judgments. Use when/ what/where/ how questions. Take note of information about Obstacles or Options but do not include them	
		Have I included facts and figures where relevant?	Facts and figures are the best kind of Reality	
		Have I included any assumptions?	Do not include information which you cannot verify	
		How many times have I tried to reach this Goal? What happened to prevent my reaching it? How do I feel about those attempts?	Include information about previous attempts at the Goal and your feelings	
		What skills, abilities and knowledge do I have that could help me?	Knowing what resources you have available is useful information	
		Is my Goal still appropriate?	Be prepeared to revise the Goal in the light of your Reality	

Stage definition	Process	Questions to consider	Hints	Chapter reference
O for Obstacles What blocks you from moving from where you are to your Goal	Consider blocks: • Within yourself • Caused by others • In the environment • Caused by a lack of resources	What is blocking me from achieving my Goal? How do I know these things are really what is blocking me? What else could be blocking me?	Give yourself the best chance of success by digging deeply to discover all your Obstacles so you can deal with them effectively	Chapter 8
		What might I have to face that I don't want to in order to achieve my Goal?	The more honest you are about your inner obstacles the easier they are to deal with. Be specific about what you are afraid of	
		How would I have to change personally in order to achieve this Goal?	Do you have any beliefs about yourself that are in the way?	
		Am I considering the current situation or being influenced by past experiences?	Look at the situation *now* – not at any previous time	
		How are other people obstructing me? Do I know why they are being obstructive or am I making an assumption?	Be as factual as you can about how other peole are obstructing you	

Stage definition	Process	Questions to consider	Hints	Chapter reference
		Do I have the right environment to achieve my Goal? What do I need that I do not have now?	Physical things can obstruct you as well as mental or emotional issues	
		What resources do I need that I do not have now? What skills, abilities or information do I need that I do not have now? Do I have the time and money to achieve my Goal?	Consider carefully what skills and resources you need that you do not currently have	
		Am I sure my Obstacle is real and not a justification?	Ensure you understand how the Obstacle is really stopping you	
		Do I face any risks or threats?	Be realistic if there are dangers	
		Is my Goal still appropriate?	Be prepared to revise the Goal in the ilght of your Obstacles	

Stage definition	Process	Questions to consider	Hints	Chapter reference
O for Options – Finding practical ways around the Obstacles	Use 'abundance thinking' Consider how change within yourself would create Options	What is the simplest solution? What would make the most difference?	Be prepared to use unusual techniques to find creative Options	
		If there were no limitations how would I handle the Obstacle?	Use questions starting with 'suppose' or 'if'	
	Use the 'selves' exercise	Is there a tried and tested way of handling this Obstacle?	Create lots of Options without judging them and select them later	
		Who do I know who could deal with this Obstacle well? How would they go about it? What mistakes have I seen others make? How could I avoid those mistakes myself?	Imagine how other people you know would create Options	
		How could I change my behaviour to get a different result? How could I find the resources I need?		
	Use your support systems to help you create Options	Who/what might be willing to help?	You can have wide ranging Options or Options which are close to action steps	
	Select the three Options that will be most effective in moving towards your Goal	Which Option would produce the best result with the least effort/resources? Which Option would be most challenging to me? Which Option is most or least like me?	Choose Options which are challenging and realistic	

Stage definition	Process	Questions to consider	Hints	Chapter reference
W is for Way Forward – The action steps you are going to take that will achieve your Goal	Processes Create an action list that you are confident you can carry out	Are my action steps in a SMART format? How confident am I that I can achieve my action steps? What bold action could I take that is different from what I normally do? Who could I ask for support and what type of support will I ask them for? Have I thought through the consequences of my action steps? How committed am I to my action steps? How could I increase my commitment?	Action steps need to be realistic or will lead to disappointment Including a bold action can greatly speed progress Make sure you include the support you will need for your actions. Ask for what you really need You could sabotage yourself if you do not plan ahead Commitment is key to carrying out actions	Chapter 11

Stage definition	Process	Questions to consider	Hints	Chapter reference
Staying Motivated How to maintain your motivation and recover it if necessary		To find the reasons you might *not* achieve your Goal complete the sentence 'I want my Goal but . . .' in as many ways as you can	Understand that everybody has low points. It is part of the process. The only way you can fail is to give up	Go for a quick solution Chapter 12
		Complete the sentence 'I want my Goal in order to . . .' to find what you really want	Watch out for any 'hidden agendas' you might have	
			Make sure your Goal will really give you what you want	
	Monitor your motivation levels		Make a graph of your motivation levels and look for patterns	
		Who would be best to support me? Who do I really want to support me?	Use your support networks at difficult times	
		Ask them for their ideas of how they could help		
	Find something that will motivate you for the next 10 minutes		Be prepared to talk to the part of you that does not want to do what is necessary for your Goal	

Stage definition	Process	Questions to consider	Hints	Chapter reference
	Allow yourself to wallow in misery for a fixed period of time	What is the smallest thing I can do that will actually move me forward?	Break the task down Forgive yourself and move on. Don't believe the thought 'This will not work for me'	

Stage definition	Process	Questions to consider	Hints	Chapter reference
Celebration	Create a celebration to mark the end of your Goal	How can I make a celebration which will truly show I have accomplished my Goal? If I usually avoid celebration how could I create an event which would reflect my Goal?	If you plan a celebration of your accomplishments you will find it pulls you towards your Goal and makes it easier to motivate yourself for your next objective!	

3

Stopping the struggle

The process of struggle
How we cause ourselves to fail
How the structure of the Goal helps or hinders us

Reading tips
Reflect on past Goals.
Take responsibility.
Learn and move on.

In our introduction we said that the GROW process would help you achieve your Goals but it needed application and perseverance to make it work. True, the process is extremely powerful but, as we discovered with the Test Team, it is not always straightforward in its application. In theory, when we want to achieve a Goal the ideal way is to sit down and map out the steps, organise ourselves to carry out the plan, put in the required effort and enjoy our reward. In practice, we are human beings, full of contradictions and counter-intentions. So, instead of moving swiftly towards our Goals, we often end up 'struggling' with ourselves.

The process of struggle

We all struggle

Throughout the eight-week project the Test Team participants experienced a lot of internal conflict. It was as if, as soon as they started to define their Goals, the part of them that did not want to move made its voice heard.

The struggle for some came at the start of the GROW process when the idea of setting a clear measurable Goal had their minds saying, 'No, let's be vague so that we don't really have to commit to this and can leave ourselves an easy way out.' For others, it was during the Reality and Obstacles stages that their negative voice was offered a platform to undermine simple facts with every type of destructive thought imaginable. These included, 'You know you do not have the self-discipline to do this,' or 'You have failed before and this is going to be yet another time,' and many more.

When the Options and Way Forward actions were being considered, the mind started saying, 'This is boring,' or 'Bob and Chris are talking about fun and creativity and that is just not me.' In essence the struggle was with the internal voices and not the actual requirements of the Goal or situations thrown up by the GROW process.

Responding to difficulty and pain

In order to understand why we find ourselves struggling, let's look at how humans and animals respond to different types of pain. We share a common reaction to move away from physical pain, but when the pain is mental we often have a different reaction to the animal world. Human beings talk about a 'painful' relationship, but it does not necessarily cause us physical pain or automatically motivate us to take action. Because we have a mind we can exhibit a greater range of behaviour than simple flight/fight responses.

This is because we can imagine what might happen in the future. We can conjure up fearful thoughts like, 'I do not want to be on my own,' 'What will my parents/friends/peers think of me if I give it up?' or 'How will I break the news to my partner?'

So, for all sorts of reasons, we often stay in painful and difficult situations because, unlike animals, we can project into the future and estimate that we might lose something if we give up the status quo. Fear and inertia hold us firmly in their grip, we are unable to move forward or back, and we end up struggling.

Wishful thinking can also play a part in keeping us stuck because we can look forward and hope that things will get better by themselves, justifying to ourselves that doing nothing is all right. We are trying to have our cake and eat it. We don't want pain but we don't want to lose anything either. Human beings have an infinite capacity for tying themselves up in knots when faced with difficult situations.

The cost of staying safe

We can be caught in this kind of trap because of the way we have dealt with problems in the past. Let's use the analogy of walking along a country path and meeting a forest that blocks our Way Forward. If we are to progress, we have to decide whether to go through it or round it. It would be quicker to go through it but that would involve effort and uncertainty. We might get lost, or it might be hard work to get through.

Being human, we often tend to stick to the known and go around the difficulty rather than face our fear and make an effort to go through it. The roundabout route may take longer, but it feels safer.

The next time we go along that path, or a similar one, and meet a forest, we are conditioned to go around it so we repeat the pattern. When we do this over and again it becomes second nature to take the route around the forest and harder and harder to pull ourselves out of the rut we create.

So we go through life avoiding the forests and following routes we know well. Some of the 'ruts' are perfectly acceptable and don't really cause us problems. For example, if you are happy for your partner to always choose your clothes there is no problem. However, suppose it was another kind of problem – perhaps an unhappy relationship or a job you dislike. If your way of handling problems is to avoid them then you may find it impossible to deal directly with the issue, even if you are in a lot of pain.

The result of this avoidance is that we find ourselves feeling like the rope in a tug-of-war, being pulled from one side to the other, not in control and feeling stuck and frustrated. We feel trapped and unable to move. To make matters worse, we often criticise ourselves for not being able to deal more effectively with the situation. This struggle takes a huge amount of energy although very little is achieved by it.

How we cause ourselves to fail

So, how does this inbuilt capacity to sabotage ourselves manifest itself when we set out to achieve Goals?

There are, we suggest, two main ways in which we can become caught up in the struggle rather than make progress:

- Our personal history and personality can hinder us.
- Our Goals can be structured in ineffective ways.

Getting in our own way

Let's consider the ways in which our beliefs and behaviours can prevent us from setting or achieving our Goals. All these issues were experienced by the Test Team in their past or over the course of the project.

Too much thinking

Too much consideration can prevent a Goal from being set and started. Paralysis by analysis is a real threat and it is often the most intelligent people who suffer from this form of extended mindplay.

One example is that by aiming for one Goal you may be closing off your other avenues. Donald knew he was unhappy as a financial advisor but could not bear the thought of even starting to look for anything else, because he believed that in doing so he would cut off his other options. The result was that he spent years thinking about what he could do without ever exploring the real possibilities.

ASK YOURSELF

Am I someone who spends more time in thought than action?

Am I a perfectionist who wants everything to be just right before venturing out?

Am I waiting until the circumstances are 'just right' or 'perfect'?

In this book we offer the opportunity to let go of this pattern and discover how you can move out of the world of thoughts and into the world of achievement.

Rushing in regardless

The opposite of holding back in thought is leaping directly into action without really considering your Reality, Obstacles and Options. This hasty approach can result in the creation of Goals which lack any real substance and cause you to fall at the first hurdle. This is a pattern that can repeat itself time and time again.

Wanting something very quickly can often lead to disappointment – and as the army saying goes, time spent in reconnaissance is seldom wasted. It is important to accept that achieving any worthwhile Goal is a step-by-step process that takes time and consideration. As Susan said, 'I have a tendency to set a Goal and think it will be really easy so there is no need to prepare, and then I wonder why it is not working when in fact I did nothing at all to make it work.'

By applying yourself within the GROW process you will have the very best chance of achieving your Goal.

'This is selfish'

You might think that setting and achieving Goals is selfish. It was certainly an issue for some of the Test Team who realised that they tended to please others and so did not go for what they really wanted.

To be in this position is rarely as altruistic as it appears. While it is good to look after the interests of others, failure to consider and nurture our own needs is ultimately a recipe for frustration and bitterness.

If you identify strongly with this:

ASK YOURSELF

How well do I look after myself generally?

The world needs people who look after themselves and others while focusing on what they want. If you still have reservations, there is nothing stopping you having a Goal which includes being of service to others.

'We are not worthy!'

One of the biggest fears that can hold us back from achieving something worthwhile is the feeling that we are somehow 'unworthy' of success. By believing we do not deserve to achieve our Goals we keep ourselves small, restrict our power and often snatch defeat from the jaws of victory. This sense of unworthiness can come from our upbringing or from harmful events that have happened in our lives and that we feel responsible for.

This type of fear is very difficult to deal with by ourselves and is one of the reasons we formed the Test Team. Alone, we can make excuses and conveniently 'forget' to do the things that we need to accomplish when moving towards our Goal. However, with others to witness and support our progress it is much harder to let actions slip. The power of the Test Team working together through each stage of the process enabled some of our participants to see for the first time how fear had been affecting their lives.

'I no longer have to be run by my fear of making mistakes and my inability to ask for what I want,' said Susan. Instead of living with frustration and excuses, the Test Team were able to genuinely choose their Goals.

'It is all too much!'

Maybe the whole idea of setting a Goal is just too much even to consider right now.

Kathy in our Test Team wrote to say, 'I have really tried to work out my Goal but am finding it too difficult. My emotional situation [with her partner] has always caused me to mess things up. I feel guilty and a failure and this is just making me feel worse.' We tried hard to get Kathy back on the programme, but her emotional needs were too deep for what we could offer.

There are genuine circumstances where other types of support, such as counselling or therapy, are more appropriate than the GROW process. However, several other Test Team participants were also in a very fragile emotional state and they did complete the programme. It is up to each person to judge whether they are ready for the emotional and physical requirements of change.

During one of the kick-off sessions for the Test Team Linda was having a lot of difficulty defining her Goals. When we asked her to think about a Goal she would like in her life she became very upset – she felt her current life was such a mess she could not bear to think about it, let alone think how it could be improved.

She said anger and fear had ruled her life and she had got into the habit of trying to control everyone and everything in order to keep them at bay. Rather than trying to force her to do something she felt unable to do, we asked if she could draw a picture of how life was for her. She drew a picture of a volcano, because often that was how she felt. Once she had created this image she was visibly calmer.

It was as if by getting a representation of her emotions down on paper, she could move on. We then asked her what she wanted to change about the picture. She said she would like to be calmer and not have to control everything. She completed the picture by drawing herself and her daughter dancing away happily into a new life. From that point she could start to think about clearer Goals, which would improve her relationships and circumstances.

Being in such a state of emotional turmoil that you do not know how or where to start is a very genuine reason for not articulating or achieving a Goal. Perhaps you bought this book precisely because you feel like that. As Linda learned, it is possible to move past this state if you have the right structure and support.

There may also be circumstances in your life which, if not addressed, will prevent a particular Goal being completed. Of course, such situations could themselves be used to create a Goal in order to clear up problem areas of your life. As you turn the pages you will not be short of ideas of how the GROW process will give you a very powerful way of taking that first important step and then moving forward.

Fear of failure or success

Many of the reasons that people do not accomplish, or even set, Goals comes down to one thing – fear. Fear can take many forms, from 'What will people think of me if I achieve, or don't achieve, my Goals?' to 'How will I cope with failure if I do not get this Goal? I would rather have it as a dream.' Fear can keep us stuck, not even daring to look at how we could move forward.

Unfortunately it is human nature to avoid fears and uncomfortable feelings rather than address them. As we have shown, this can become a pattern affecting all aspects of your life. If you do not believe it, try this simple test.

Discovery Exercise 1: Fear of success or failure

Objective: To identify feelings around going for Goals

1 Think of a very significant Goal you would like to accomplish.
2 Imagine you have the world's best Goal coach by your side, saying, 'Right, tomorrow you are going to start working towards your Goal. I am not going to do it for you but I will make sure you do all the things you need to reach your Goal. No more excuses, tomorrow is the day!'

ASK YOURSELF

Do I just have a feeling of excitement and anticipation or is there also a twinge of fear about what I might now have to face to achieve my Goal?

Caroline was an actress and a very talented one, but she had not been getting the parts she wanted. When she first joined the Test Team she set herself an exciting Goal of receiving a call offering her a major TV or film part. In the next couple of weeks we did not hear much from her. However, when we started looking at the Obstacles she had an important insight.

While the Goal was initially exciting for her, she now felt 'numb' and could not get energised at the prospect of achieving it. She realised that she was avoiding the GROW process, because if she did take charge and it did not work out it would mean that she was a complete failure! So it was safer not to ask for what she wanted from her agent and casting directors because then she did not have to risk being disappointed. It is extremely debilitating to believe that our actions could confirm our worst secret fears.

Interestingly, while on stage she loved playing dark, powerful women, but she shrank away from applying that power to her everyday life. Once she realised how she was inhibiting herself she was no longer bound by her fear.

The fear of failure can control us in very insidious ways. Often we are simply not aware of how our fears are holding us back. We find ourselves avoiding starting our Goals, or feeling that they are just too much effort or trouble.

Molly's Goal seemed very straightforward when she first brought it to the Test Team. She had been working on a novel that she had half written. Her Goal was to have a first draft finished by the end of the Test Team programme. She recognised that she sabotaged herself by not planning things properly. However, the real problem was her fear about showing the completed book to someone, in her case her husband. 'Suppose I show it to him and he thinks it is rubbish? What will I do then?' she said. Up to that point her fear of judgement had kept the book unfinished.

Goals, by their very nature, take you rapidly from the general to the very specific, and with this focus and clarity comes fear. Many fears can be dealt with simply by a decision to commit to achieving your Goal, although of course this is not always easy.

Indeed, lack of commitment is probably the main reason why Goals do not get fully formed or completed.

The enormity of some Goals, particularly if they relate to decisions such as leaving or building a life with a partner, can be quite overwhelming. We were moved to see the way some Test Team participants took up this challenge and the huge insights they gained in doing so. We hope that as you read their stories they will inspire you to look at the challenges you face in your life.

We often find ourselves wobbling on top of the fence, trapped between the frustration of not moving forward and the fear of actually doing so. One participant summed up the move from comfort into commitment when she said, 'I am going to have to do it now and I have never been so afraid and excited in my life!'

ASK YOURSELF

How do I respond to the challenge of commitment?

If this is an issue for you, then can you commit to yourself and maybe to others that you will stay with this book and the GROW process? There will be an opportunity to make this commitment in the next chapter.

'They' won't let me succeed

Lack of support and even active hostility from people around us can often prevent us from pushing on with our Goals. Whether we like it or not, our close friends and family often have a vested interest in us staying just the way we are. If we start to change it is only human nature for them to worry about the effect it will have on them. Unconsciously they might even sabotage or hinder our progress because they feel threatened.

It would be ideal if our Goals were not only in our best

interests but also in the best interests of those around us. This can sometimes be the case, but in other instances it may not be. Since support is very important we must be careful to choose the individuals who are most likely to help us achieve our Goals. You will see we place great emphasis on creating effective support structures in this book, as well as helping you to ask for what you need from others.

Voices from the past

As you have seen at the start of this chapter, our internal dialogue can have a far greater impact on our failure to achieve Goals than anything we encounter externally. For example, we can tell ourselves that we are too old or too young to achieve what we want. One participant in the Test Team believed that she had the 'wrong education' to achieve her Goal. When we asked her what she meant by that and how it stopped her, she could not say, but until we asked she was convinced that it was a real Obstacle. Another recalled that her mother used to say, 'What guarantee have you got that this will work?'

We often hear these types of patterns in the language we use, such as 'I always . . .' or 'I never . . .' and 'I'm not the sort of person who . . .' These generalisations from the past can actually result in you running your life based on something you were told and believed many years ago. With the GROW process these outdated messages and limiting beliefs can be seen for what they are and you can decide not to have your future dictated by your past.

ASK YOURSELF

Was there someone in my life, particularly in my child-hood days, who told me that I would not make a success of something or that 'people like us' just did not do things like that?

Many of us can recall an experience that has left its mark on our present thinking about what we can or cannot accomplish. These self-imposed constraints are rarely actual barriers, although they can seem very real. Take some quiet time now to consider your 'story' and how it might limit what you allow yourself to achieve.

How the structure of the Goal helps or hinders us

Now that we have examined our personal blocks to achieving Goals, let's look at how the structure of the Goal itself can assist or hinder our progress. As you read through, you can check to see if any of the sections apply to Goals that you might have set in the past.

Where does this Goal get me?

Sometimes we do not set or achieve Goals because we are not clear what difference achieving the Goal would really make. This is particularly true for Goals of obligation or duty, where we feel that we *should* achieve something rather than that we *want* to achieve it.

Goals which can be expressed very simply, such as weight loss or becoming calmer, can dramatically change many aspects of our lives. By recognising this *before* you start, you increase the potential impact of the Goal and your motivation to achieve it.

In the GROW process we help you get fully in touch with the benefits and values of your chosen Goal. We will also be showing you how achieving the Goal will actually look and feel before you even start out, so you can be sure it is something you really want.

'I'm not leaving until I know how to get there'

A common reason for not achieving a specific Goal is that it was not particularly well thought through in the first place. As the saying goes, if we fail to plan we plan to fail. Achieving anything worthwhile takes a lot of planning and you need a good structure.

'I have never really been able to see just one small step at a time – until now. Sometimes it doesn't help to look at the big picture. I frequently put off taking things any further because I want to see the route before I have decided on the destination. It's safer, of course, to do nothing at all. No wonder I feel frustrated and that I'm underachieving,' commented Susan.

It is important to plan our route in advance. By doing so we might discover that we lack the skills to achieve something. Having recognised this we can then take action to address this gap. There could be destructive patterns which, if not acknowledged, will hold us back time and time again. There are many ways of achieving the same thing, but we will only discover them if we take time to look for them. With good planning we can take all this into account and our chances of success are greatly increased.

Just too many Goals

Do you suffer from having too many Goals? If you do, then maybe this is a subtle form of sabotage, as you have created a good excuse for not achieving any of them. Setting a Goal certainly focuses your attention on achieving one thing at one time.

We would like to invite you to decide on the priorities in your life – what is really important to you or the 'difference which will make the difference'. There are only twenty-four hours in a day and, assuming that you do not have copious amounts of free time, any Goal that you set will have to compete with all your other activities.

If you are currently learning to play the piano, work out regularly and spend time in the garden, something might have to take a back seat if you also want to, say, build a website. There is, of course, no harm in ringing the changes and dropping something for a time while you pursue other interests.

We would also mention a phenomenon that occurred in the Test Team and which we came to describe as 'Goal Creep'. This can happen in two ways.

The first way is that when you start the GROW process you discover another deeper and bigger Goal under your original Goal. For example, your Goal could be to learn a new language. When you start to explore this Goal you realise that learning a new language would open up the possibility of moving to a country where that language is spoken, an idea which appeals to you. So you change your Goal to moving to that country. However, being able to move would depend on your relationship with your spouse, who does not like change. So you change your Goal again to resolving that issue. From a comparatively simple Goal you go deeper into problems which become progressively more difficult and intractable. The end result is that it becomes hard or impossible to make progress because the Goal has become so enormous it cannot be dealt with.

The other way that 'Goal Creep' happens is that you set a Goal and then start to think 'This is not enough.' Perhaps you compare yourself to other people in this book or hear about other people's Goals and start to think, 'I want that, too!' The result is that you take on so many Goals you cannot give sufficient attention to any of them.

The solution to the problem of 'Goal Creep' is to select one Goal which feels a challenge but does not overwhelm you. It is not a good idea to try and sort out the deepest challenge or all your life issues in one go. While there is nothing wrong with looking at deeper and more important Goals, the experience of many in the Test Team was that working on one Goal that was attainable had a beneficial effect on the deeper Goals.

Starting to make progress in one area gives a clearer

understanding of what the 'real' situation is, which in turn helps resolve the deeper issues. So in our example above, by starting to learn the language we might come into contact with natives of that country, which will help us decide if we want to move there.

We will help you choose the Goal which is best for you right now. Also, once you have used and understood GROW to get your first Goal you can always use the process to achieve more.

'It is beyond my control'

It could be argued that all Goals are to some extent 'in the lap of the gods'. For example, you could have achieved a Goal to get an exciting new job, and then get run down by a bus before your first day. You might like to set a Goal to win the Lottery, but that is something you cannot make happen. So some Goals are more in your control than others.

In pursuing any Goal, however rational, there will almost certainly be some elements beyond your control. However, this is no argument for not setting Goals at all. There are no absolute guarantees in the Goal-setting business except that no Goal means no gain. It is also true that the greater the degree of control you have over the outcome, the more likely you are to achieve the Goal.

One area where we do have more control is with 'personal process Goals'. This is where, instead of setting a Goal, to, say, 'win an Olympic gold medal', we aim to beat our own personal best time. With 'personal process Goals' there is far more control, although even then you cannot guarantee you will succeed.

As you work through this book, we will help you choose Goals that are reasonably within your control.

'It is just too big'

Sometimes a Goal can be just too big or too much of a stretch to reach in one go. We risk becoming totally overwhelmed by the enormity of the Goal, losing motivation and intention along the way. Breaking Goals down into smaller chunks or sub Goals makes achieving them much more manageable.

Jean wanted to write a travel book, but she was finding the GROW process a real challenge until she had a breakthrough.

> My friends suggested I just get the travel article I had planned written and published! It was the idea I needed. It might seem a small Goal, but now I'm inspired. I already have all the notes, the ideas, the photos, even the laptop. When I was trying to get my book published, I just never seemed to have made the time.

By breaking the Goal into something more manageable Jean could see a way through. Once her article has been published she will be able to show potential book publishers and agents that her travel writing has already been in the media. This was a significant first step in moving forward as a travel writer.

No reference points

We show you in this book how to create milestones that will mark your progress towards your Goal. We all need some reference points to demonstrate our successes along the way. In a past life as a business manager, Chris often used to remind his sales team that they needed as many camps from the bottom to the top of the revenue mountain as possible. This meant that they could open a bottle of champagne at Camp One, Camp Two, Camp Three and so on, rather than waiting until they had made it to the top. That way, the journey was much more motivational and enjoyable as there were far more opportunities for recognition.

To set milestones, your Goal also has to be easily measured, with definite start and finish points. Ongoing, open-ended Goals with no strong indicators of success are far more likely to fail, as there is nothing to aim for and no way of knowing when you get there.

As you work through this book we will provide you with many exciting ways of quantifying your Goal. In this way you will have absolutely no doubt when you have achieved it.

Is this the 'wrong' Goal?

There is probably no such thing as a 'wrong' Goal, as every experience involves some learning and often our mistakes can teach us more than our successes. However, a poorly considered 'half-hearted' Goal fails to capture our interest and energy and we quickly lose impetus and give up. On the other hand, a really motivational Goal with solid benefits stands the best chance of capturing all our attention and effort. Let's face it, achieving a worthwhile Goal is difficult enough, so why not choose a Goal that has your full buy-in?

Often a Goal might seem casually appealing. It might be great to be one of the contestants on a TV 'reality' show and have a lot of screaming media attention for a few weeks. But then how would you cope when it was all over? Would you really be a happier person, or feel lost and forgotten when you had to return to everyday life?

When we look at our Goals it is very important to consider how exactly we would benefit by achieving the Goal. Otherwise we could find ourselves pursuing something for the wrong reasons or being disappointed when it does not give us what we hoped for.

As coaches, we hold our clients fully capable of anything they want to achieve – but let's face it, your Goal might actually be unrealistic. There is a wonderful TV sketch with Peter Cook and Dudley Moore. 'Dud' is auditioning for the role of Tarzan while hopping around the stage on one leg. As 'Pete' says, 'To my mind the British public is not ready for the sight of a one-legged ape-man swinging through the jungly tendrils.' But there is still hope: 'Failing two-legged actors, you, a unidexter, are just the sort of person we shall be attempting to contact telephonically.'

Just don't set a Goal!

A great way of avoiding the disappointment associated with failing to achieve a Goal is not to set one in the first place. By not setting a Goal we can successfully avoid feelings that we might not be comfortable with.

As Tiffany in the Test Team discovered, setting a Goal can bring up feelings you have been avoiding. Her Goal was 'An apartment with clear surfaces, ordered drawers, no piles of paper or clothes anywhere, a wardrobe of clothes that I actually wear, and a place for everything'.

> This sounded like quite an achievable and simple Goal until I started to think about it in more detail, and actually now it seems very big and quite scary. The piles of stuff have been my shield against the outside world, and envisioning a clear apartment makes me feel very naked, exposed and vulnerable. There is a feeling that there will be no more excuses for me not to live a full life, and that I am hiding behind the fact that I don't have the time and energy to sort out the basics of life, let alone arrange a fulfilling social life, etc.

As she reflected on the Goal she discovered more about why she had not achieved it in the past.

Life itself can also make a Goal seem irrelevant. In a Test Team kick-off workshop, Michelle mentioned that she was just too bogged down with everyday life, taking care of family, home and work, to set Goals. We fully understand this feeling, but we all need something to look forward to whatever our circumstances. Setting Goals, however small, offers us an opportunity to break out of the old routines and create something really different.

If we continually fail to take charge of our lives in a positive way we feel frustrated and dissatisfied. These feelings are like barnacles on a ship's hull, draining our energy and slowing our progress through the waters of life. Simply by starting out on our Goal we release pent-up energy that can be used to propel us forward.

Now it's your turn

You have just read about some of the ways we struggle and fail to achieve our Goals. Now we are going to ask you to consider:

• What Goals have you set in the past and failed to achieve?
• Why might that have happened?
• Do you set Goals at all?
• If not, what holds you back?

It is important to be honest. If you understand why you don't set and achieve Goals, you can choose Goals that are more likely to be successful. You will then be more aware, as you go through the GROW process, of the type of problems that can occur for you.

**Discovery Exercise 2:
Why have I struggled with Goals in the past?**

Objective: To identify why I have failed to achieve Goals in the past

Review the material in this chapter and list the five main reasons why you do not set or reach your Goals.

1
2
3
4
5

4

Preparing the ground

Developing the right environment
Creating a support structure
Keeping track of your progress
Your past history with Goals

Reading tips
Prepare thoroughly.
Be realistic.
Try new ideas and suggestions.

Developing the right environment

Doing the groundwork

If we are to grow carrots we first have to prepare the ground.
This can be hard work. However, the more effort we put into
this 'groundwork' the better our crop will be. In the same way,
if we are to grow our motivational carrots, we have to prepare
the ground before we begin the GROW process.

If our minds are not clear and focused our whole approach

to the Goal will be muddled and half-hearted and, as we have seen, there are many deep-rooted reasons why some of us do not achieve what we want. In this chapter we will help you assemble everything you need to ensure that the progress towards your Goal will be a success, not a struggle.

Do you have the time?

It takes time to achieve anything new. If your days are already full, you will have to take account of that in planning to achieve your Goal. Just reading through this book will take a few hours, let alone answering the many questions and working through the exercises. It is important, therefore, to consider whether you really have the time right now to make the GROW process effective for you.

Lack of time was a key reason why some Test Team participants failed to achieve their Goals. The GROW process requires commitment. For those who participated fully the project took up a significant amount of time and occupied an important part of their daily life.

If your Goal is really important to you then you are more likely to prioritise it and give it the time required. If time is an issue for you we suggest you allow sufficient time to read the book, pick a simple Goal to achieve and do just some of the Discovery Exercises and *ASK YOURSELF* exercises. When you have achieved your Goal you will have a good understanding of how the GROW process works in practice. You can then apply it to achieve more complex Goals.

Of course, you might have bought this book with the intention of working on a huge burning Goal for which you are fully prepared to make a big time commitment. If this is the case then that is fantastic, and we promise we will make the time you spend on this process well worthwhile.

> *ASK YOURSELF*
>
> Am I prepared to make the minimum time available to give this book and the GROW process a fair trial?

If the answer to this question is 'no' then maybe you should consider setting a future date when you will have the time available.

As well as putting the time aside to work on your Goal, we also suggest you set a specific time frame for its completion. For the Test Team we chose eight weeks, but certainly twelve is the absolute maximum we would recommend.

Creating a productive environment

If you are going to give this book the very best chance of success, then it is important to create an environment which will allow you to do what is required to complete the GROW process.

You should also consider the impact going for your Goal will have on others. Those living alone might well have the advantage here, but if you have a partner and perhaps children, your Goal-getting could impact on them. Even if there is not a time consideration it will be helpful to explain your Goal and its implications to your partner so that you have their support and understanding.

We appreciate that creating an environment to support your Goal might well be part of the Goal itself. However, if your Goal is large we would certainly advise considering the resources the Goal requires before you go for it, rather than encountering them when you get to the Obstacles stage of the process. Here is a quick quiz to test whether your environment is well prepared.

Discovery Exercise 1: Environmental audit

Objective: To check out whether you have the best environment for Goal-getting

Take some quiet time to answer the following questions. Don't think too much when completing them, as it is a fun exercise and your first answer is probably the best.

1 I have a clear and tidy space to work in:
   a ☐ Ask for anything I'll tell you where it is.
   b ☐ I did my filing a week ago.
   c ☐ Give me a few minutes, I can find it.
   d ☐ If I could see my desk I'd tell you.

2 I know how to work productively:
   a ☐ You *can* have it yesterday.
   b ☐ You can have it today.
   c ☐ Would a few days be OK?
   d ☐ OK, I will let you have it sometime.

3 I have the time available that my Goal needs:
   a ☐ I always create the time I need.
   b ☐ I could create a couple of spare hours this week.
   c ☐ I only have a few spare minutes at the moment.
   d ☐ You must be kidding. Me? Spare time?

4 I am in charge of my money:
   a ☐ Money is my friend.
   b ☐ I can tell you roughly what I have in the bank.
   c ☐ I worry about money.
   d ☐ I don't open letters from the bank.

5 My husband/wife/partner supports me in achieving Goals:
   a ☐ We are like one Goal-getting unit.
   b ☐ S/he helps me if s/he has the time.
   c ☐ S/he does not get in the way – much.
   d ☐ Who? Oh, her/him!

6 I don't make excuses about achieving Goals:
  a ☐ It is all down to me.
  b ☐ I can do it with a bit of luck.
  c ☐ I am not a lucky sort of person.
  d ☐ I know I am too old/overweight/unattractive/
        unintelligent (insert your version here).

So how did you do? Here is the scoring key:

For each (a) answer score 1 point.
For each (b) answer score 2 points.
For each (c) answer score 3 points.
For each (d) answer score 4 points.

If you scored between 6 and 10 – you should be writing this book.
If you scored between 11 and 15 – you are on the starting blocks.
If you scored between 16 and 20 – you should read the preparation notes again.
If you scored between 21 and 24 – perhaps this is not the right time to be Goal-setting.

Creating a support structure

Why support is so valuable

Scoring goals on the football pitch takes outstanding players, inspirational management, great facilities and lots and lots of cash. However, one key ingredient for any successful sporting club is the fans: the 'barmy armies' who, come rain or shine, pack the terraces, to cheer on the team and their favourite players. As Sir Alex Ferguson, manager of Manchester United Football Club, says, 'Without the fans the game is nothing. What would be the point?'

The fans can make the difference between winning and losing, and they can be quite awe-inspiring. Kevin Keegan said, 'The only thing I fear is missing an open goal in front of the home fans. I would die if that were to happen.' Besides making the difference at home, a loyal fan club also makes the trip to cheer their side on, whether the away game is the other side of town or the other side of the world.

The Test Team worked so well precisely because it was a team. Everyone participating in the project had forty others to cheer them on. It was amazing to see how quickly a valuable community built up. Whatever the issue, team participants had something to contribute from their experience or knew someone who could help.

Creating a 'support club'

We would like you to consider recruiting your own support club – a group of friends who are there to lift your game and to cheer you on as you work through this book and score your Goal. Like their sporting team equivalent, they will also be there for you if you hit problems. Here's how you do it.

Discovery Exercise 2: Recruiting your 'support club'

Objective: To add the vital encouragement and advice of others as you work through this book

1   Draw up a list of six people who you would like to be in your personal support club. You need only five, but let's assume one will not want to do it for some reason. (If you get stuck, think about who has helped you in the past when you needed it. Can you ask them again or find someone like them?)

2   Beside each name write a list of the qualities you value in that person. This is what you would like them

---

to contribute as you progress through the GROW process.

3 Phone them to say what you are doing and how you value them, and to ask them if they would be willing to support you. This can be done by email, but a personal approach is better in the first instance.

4 When you receive their replies, thank them for agreeing to support you and offer your support in return for anything they might want to achieve. Maybe you can give your support group a name which it can be known by.

5 As soon as possible, arrange for you all to meet so you can tell them about this exciting project and discuss your Goal.

Once you have created this group, you need to keep them interested and engaged while you are achieving your Goal. If it is a mutual support group then you have your Goals as a point of common interest, so maintaining the community will be relatively easy. If this is a group you have created to support you and your Goal, you have to think what is in it for them, apart from supporting a friend.

Guidelines for support groups

- Make sure you communicate with the support group regularly – at least once a week.
- Give the group a name so there is an identity.
- Make the interactions fun and interesting.
- Try to make any meetings unusual and stimulating. This is an opportunity to show your creativity.
- Give everyone an opportunity to talk about what is going on with them, too.

- Be clear about the topics you want to discuss so they know where they are being asked to contribute.
- Maybe establish a theme for a particular discussion and see how everyone relates to this and their experiences.
- Always remember to thank everyone for participating.
- When acknowledging individuals try to pick a particular contribution they made so it is specific and not just a general thank you.

You can learn a great deal about yourself simply by setting up a support group and being open to others helping you.

Once you have achieved your Goal, maybe you can reverse the process and support someone else in the group to achieve theirs. Maybe you could establish a regular group that supports one member at a time to achieve a Goal every eight weeks by rotation.

Working with a buddy

If you do decide to have a buddy it is probably best if that person is also working on a Goal. This means you have a joint interest in being heard and supported. Here is what two of the Test Team said about the buddy support they received:

> Before I started on the programme I was very poor at asking for support. Having to speak to a buddy almost means having to report to someone and that in itself helps tremendously.
>
> Vanessa

> The buddy process has helped me realise how much I expect to do things by and for myself but how much better I can work by using this support.
>
> Mia

If you and your buddy are working on each other's Goals it is essential that you communicate effectively together to ensure there is a good balance of time and attention for you both. Here are some guidelines for your buddy review sessions, which should be held at least weekly:

Buddy review guidelines

1 Give equal time to both buddies – this is important to prevent one buddy missing out on support.

2 Start by having each buddy review the Goal(s) they have set and how they are doing in achieving them.

3 If your buddy is starting to take action, find out how he is doing in carrying out his action steps.

4 The chances are there will be some actions which are a stretch or difficult for him. Often these are the ones that are not completed. You can work with your buddy to help him find ways forward.

5 If your buddy is stuck in the process, or not moving forward, ask him to explain to you how and where he is stuck and then use the GROW process to help clarify how he might move forward.

6 If he has achieved his Goal you can use GROW to help him to set a new one.

Here are some simple 'Dos' and 'Don'ts' to make working with your buddy more effective!

Dos

• Be interested and excited about your buddy's Goals – not in an artificial way but by showing you are there for him.

- Believe in your buddy's ability to achieve his Goals, even if he is not completely sure of his own ability to achieve them.
- Be prepared to discuss whether it is the right Goal for him.
- Acknowledge him for the progress he has made.
- Keep the sessions confidential.
- Be prepared to put extra effort into keeping the contact with your buddy going. You may have to ring him even if he should have contacted you. If you both make the effort there is less danger of either person giving up.
- Think how you can support your buddy apart from just following the GROW process. Be prepared to go the extra mile. For example, unexpected greeting cards or emails can really make a difference to someone's day.
- Ask him to support you in the way you would like. We all wish that people would telepathically understand what we need, but in practice we have to ask. So if you need a check-in call or email each day, try asking for it.
- Use your own knowledge and life experience to help him.

Don'ts

- Don't fall into the trap of just sympathising with your buddy. Of course empathy and understanding are important, but the focus of the session should be how to help him find a Way Forward.
- Don't assume that you know how he feels or what he should be doing.
- Don't give too many suggestions or give advice before he has had an opportunity to think through the situation himself using GROW. Your job is to facilitate rather than provide answers. In the long term it is much more effective. If you allow him to find his own answers he will be much more committed to take action and more empowered than if you give him the solution.
- Don't feel you have to rescue your buddy. Trust that you can support him to find his own Way Forward.

If the relationship is not working

- Be honest and address the situation with your buddy without blaming yourself or him.
- Ask yourself if any of the issues you have about your buddy reflect an issue you have yourself.
- Be prepared to ask him for feedback about how you are doing as his buddy.
- Maybe both refer to an objective third party for advice.

To make the buddy process work you will need a minimum commitment of an hour a week to give to your buddy. This will mean arranging that time in advance. These sessions should be conducted over the phone or face to face, although it is possible to have a chat on a web messenger service like Yahoo or MSN if this is your preference.

Choosing the support which will work best for you

There are a number of options for creating a support network:

- Have a 'support club' around you who are not getting Goals themselves.
- Form a mutual support group with several people, all of whom are going for their Goals.
- Work closely with just one buddy and have a 'support club' of others who give you support in other ways.
- Work closely with just one buddy and no 'support club'.
- Have a buddy who is also going for a Goal and support each other through the process.
- Have your buddy just support you and consider supporting them later when they want to go for a Goal.

Each Option has its own benefits, and it depends on how you work best. The Test Team had a buddy and the support of the rest of the group, with everyone going for a Goal. This proved to be a powerful combination, although not everybody can arrange that degree of support.

ASK YOURSELF

Which support structure am I going to choose and work with?
How am I going to set it up?
When am I going to set it up?

Keeping track of your progress

All great journeys are recorded in some way. Every ship has a log, and the diaries of great explorers have us enthralled long after they have taken their last step. We suggest you set up a folder in which you can record your insights and learning as you progress towards your Goal. Here is a checklist for what it should contain:

Checklist for your GROW folder	✓
A detailed description of your Goal and defining moment	
A description of what it will mean to you when you have achieved this Goal • what people will say about you; • what you will be able to do that you could not do before; • how you will feel about yourself.	
Pictures that symbolise your Goal – either from a paper or magazine or drawn yourself	

Inspirational cards and quotes	
Contact numbers for your support club and buddies	
To-do lists	
Calendar	
A plan for what you will do if you are slipping or becoming demotivated	
Descriptions of key milestones	
Ways of monitoring your progress, such as charts and graphs	
A letter to you written by a 'future you' to offer congratulations on achieving your Goal	
Descriptions of how you are going to celebrate when you achieve your milestones and final Goal	

We appreciate that some of you might like to open an electronic folder. This could contain all the written information above but in electronic form, plus:

Pictures from the Web that symbolise your Goal or photos that you have in digital form	
Emails and contact numbers for your support club and buddies in an easy-to-access program	
Project management tools that could help you monitor your progress	
To-do lists and calendar – perhaps using Outlook or a similar tool	
A list of websites (including ours) that can provide inspiration or support	

One important ingredient for your folder should be a journal which you complete every day. Matthew, one of the most successful Test Team members, wrote an online journal for the whole period of the project. He found that when he hit Obstacles it really supported him in staying focused and finding a way through. In addition, other team members were able to read it and offer support.

Journal-writing hints

- Write in your journal at a regular time each day. The end of the day is probably best but any time which works for you is fine.
- Record details of any significant events that changed how you felt about the GROW process.
- Explore what you can learn about yourself from the things you remember.
- Write freely for ten minutes while thinking about where you are with your Goal.
- Develop some themes which are important for you, such as your fears, or different ways to have fun, or seeing how often a story from the past comes up for you.
- Reread what you wrote on other days to see if you can discern patterns about what helps or hinders you on your journey.

The journal is a great document to refer to after you have achieved your Goal, or when you are down, to see what progress you have made. It also demonstrates how our feelings can change from day to day.

Your past history with Goals

The Goal preparation audit

Finally, in terms of preparation, it is a good idea to consider your past track record in achieving Goals. Think of this as a soil test to see what type of ground we are going to start with as we grow those motivational carrots.

Discovery Exercise 3: Goal preparation audit

Objective: To see how prepared you are for starting the GROW process

Answer the following questions as honestly as you can.

1 Do you set clear Goals in your life?
   ☐ Never
   ☐ Sometimes
   ☐ Often
   ☐ Always.

2 Do you find setting Goals
   ☐ Very easy
   ☐ Easy
   ☐ Hard
   ☐ Very hard?

3 Do you find achieving Goals
   ☐ Very easy
   ☐ Easy
   ☐ Hard
   ☐ Very hard?

4 If you have never set Goals before, what has stopped you? For example: fear of failure, lack of support, not knowing what you want, fear of the unknown.

---

5 What are the main difficulties (if any) you have had in the past when achieving Goals? For example: lack of persistence, interference from other people, not having enough time or money, setbacks occurring.

6 What are some typical Goals you have set and achieved in the past?

7 What inner qualities do you believe you have which will help you in achieving your Goal? For example: patience, persistence, willingness to learn, adaptability.

8 Given that achieving any significant Goal will require some resources, what resources are you prepared to give to support yourself in the programme? For example: time to achieve your Goal, money to support yourself, intellectual effort, physical space to work in.

We hope you have learnt a great deal by reviewing your past experience and you have identified some of the qualities and resources that either support or hinder you in the GROW process.

Having prepared the ground, you are now ready to move on to pick a topic for the Goal you are going to work with throughout this book.

5

Goal types and topics

Understanding the different types of Goal
Turning problems into projects

Reading tips
Be open to Goal possibilities.
Go for what you truly want.
Make a decision.

Understanding the different types of Goal

Almost anything can be formed into a Goal, providing you
have a clear outcome and a process for getting there. Here we
outline some very different types of Goals and show you how
they can be structured for maximum success.

Practical Goals

The simplest form of Goal is something you want to do or
achieve in your life: lose weight, learn a language, get a new
job . . . You can easily see such a Goal having a definable result

in terms of lost weight, linguistic fluency or an improved occupation. These Goals are often the easiest to focus on, not only in terms of desired outcome, but also in terms of how far you have got towards achieving them.

A wardrobe full of clothes you cannot get into, not being understood or a job you hate are all very clear invitations to make some change. This is not to say that these 'simple' *doing* Goals like weight loss or giving up smoking are always easy to achieve. If the Test Team is typical, we discovered that the simpler the Goal the more issues lay behind it. There is some logic in this, for if these aspirations were so straightforward then they would be more easily accomplished.

The Goal for Deborah was to reduce the clutter in her cupboards and drawers by 30 per cent, which sounded pretty straightforward until she explained that every room in her house had too much in it, including the attic and cellar. She had been trying to throw things out for six years but had never got very far. She made great progress initially and then she wrote to us: 'Last Friday, when I was selecting which dresses I would keep, I suddenly felt very sad and started crying without any reason.'

She found throwing things out was really hard for her because she had suffered many losses of family members and beloved pets that she had not been ready for. So what seemed to be a simple Goal was overlaid with emotional significance for her. She was reluctant to continue the throwing-out process, because it reminded her so much of forced separation.

Vanessa's Goal was to get a well-paid job in the City, similar to the position she had left six months previously in order to go travelling. Being a financial trader had been very stress-ful, which is why she had to leave, but she now wanted to go back and was finding the rigours of the job search very difficult.

'I dream of working in a place where I would be able to express my creative side,' she said when we asked what she really wanted. Her self-confidence had fallen dramatically and she was finding it hard to motivate herself. She then felt guilty for not making more effort to get a job.

We pointed out that she was caught in a vicious circle of not doing anything and then beating herself up for her inactivity. We suggested she free herself up by letting go of the current job hunt for a while and creating a Goal about finding work where she could use what she felt passionate about, like her creativity.

Interestingly, with this choice she revised her opinions about working in the City and her job search. She realised that there was a lot of creativity in her former environment, particularly if she could reduce the self-imposed stress. With this altered approach she managed to get a job back with her old employer, and we supported her in forming a Goal about managing the work without becoming over-stressed.

In later chapters we look at the fears that lie behind seemingly quite simple Goals and show you how to create Options that will have you courageously moving forward.

Material Goals

We can all immediately think of things we would like to have in our life: that new house or car, a fancy watch or a friendly pet. Sometimes it can feel as if our life is not complete until we own these things, the sense of wanting is so strong. Chris remembers every Christmas when he was a child holding the turkey wishbone and asking the Universe for the electric train set he failed to get year after year. We are sure you have similar childhood memories.

The GROW process can be used to provide a structured way of bringing material things into our lives, but it also has other benefits. For example, we can use it to identify what these possessions really give us. Often there is an underlying need which, if better understood, could lead to important insights.

When we do finally get the things we want, they can be a bitter disappointment and not live up to our expectations. The marketing people have a lovely phrase for this. They call it PPR – Post Purchase Remorse. It's that 'Oh dear, what have I done, how could I have been so stupid?' feeling.

If we simply want some new clothes then no further soul-searching is required, but if we believe a new sports car will make us more socially popular it is worth looking deeper. Addressing what we want in other ways might be more effective.

ASK YOURSELF

What would I like to have in my life right now?
What do these desires say about me, my current situation and circumstances?

If you are short of ideas then there are some great questions to stimulate your thoughts in the next chapter.

Decision Goals

We all have decisions we need to make in our lives. Maybe decision-making is a real issue for you and your life is cluttered with unfinished business. Just think how relieved you would be if these decisions were made. Or perhaps there is one huge decision you need to make which would free you up to live your life to the full. If you think of this issue now you can probably feel the physical and mental drain it has on your energy.

The key to understanding decision Goals is to say that at the end of the GROW process you will have decided which Option you will choose, rather than just evaluated the various Options you have available.

Chris remembers strolling with a friend along the Thames just after finally making a decision to end a relationship which had been unsatisfactory for a number of years. His friend said, 'Chris, do you know you are even walking differently? You are walking straight when previously you were bent over!' We can be literally loaded down by the burden of unresolved decisions in our lives.

ASK YOURSELF

How easy do I find making decisions?
Do I move through them effortlessly or do they hang around weighing me down?

We know that the longer a decision goes unmade, the harder it is to resolve. Living with a big unresolved decision can become a way of life, but certainly not a satisfactory one.

Being Goals

There is a saying that we are human beings not human doings, but if we are continually so busy *doing* things we have little time for *being*. However, the quality of how we are as people directly affects everything we do.

For example, if we are never still or at peace within ourselves, then our actions will probably be frenetic and unfocused and our relationships, both with ourselves and with others, are most likely to be poor. If we have low self-esteem and lack belief in our skills and talents, then our ability to achieve significant Goals is greatly reduced. So by setting a *being* Goal we can positively affect many areas of our lives.

We saw the value of a being Goal with Paul, a high-flyer in a global technology IT company. He was feeling the pressure of a demanding environment, both mentally and physically. The stress had become so bad he had developed heart palpitations as a consequence. He felt his communications in his job were confused and described work life as 'sprinting rather than running'. He spoke about 'expecting the finish line in another 20 metres and convincing myself that I can manage just one more sprint'. He knew the 'line' was an illusion, but he could not change his response to the pressure. His state of mind was badly affecting both his job and his hobby of amateur dramatics.

Paul needed some calm in his life, and this became the focus for a being Goal. By becoming calmer he could make clearer decisions, improve his mental and physical health and have more fulfilling relationships.

In order to make the Goal measurable we asked Paul how he would know he had succeeded. He decided on a Goal which read, 'In the last week of the GROW project and for one month afterwards I will have no stress-related heart murmurs.' If he achieved this he knew he would also have gained the state of calmness he badly needed.

He now had a clear point to work towards, and all the issues that were causing him stress could be addressed while working towards that Goal. One month after the project he had suffered no more heart murmurs and his new state of calmness had dramatic benefits for both his work and his hobby.

ASK YOURSELF

Which personal belief would be most useful for me to change?

Which personal behaviour would be most useful for me to change?

If I made that change what tangible benefit would it bring me?

How would it improve the quality of my life and my relationships?

What would others see that would demonstrate I had changed?

Perhaps after considering these questions you might want to set a being Goal to achieve through the GROW process.

Turning problems into projects

Problems, choices and decisions are of course all closely related. With any problem there are a number of choices, and this requires some sort of decision. One way of moving forward with a problem is to change its identity by making it into a project. This is also how you turn what is probably a cause for grumbling into a Goal which can be a cause for celebration.

What is a problem?

Most of us like reading about other people's problems. The word 'problem' is linked to anything which is difficult, painful or misunderstood, such as 'problem children', 'problem hair', 'drug problem', 'money problem' and so on. Labelling something a problem usually implies it is stuck in some way, but does not tell us much about what is really going on. There is no information which would help us resolve the issue.

One strategy would be to probe the problem with questions, but coming up with answers is not always that easy. For example, suppose someone is stuck in a job they hate – most people would agree that constitutes a problem. However, if we were to ask, 'Well what sort of job would you like to do?' many individuals would not be able to tell you about an alternative job they wanted. Their focus is on the problems with their current role.

A case study

We can illustrate this point with a dialogue from an actual coaching session. Bob once coached a single parent called Peter who had a 'problem child' called Jane. He had been a single parent for many years and had coped well up to now. When Jane reached the age of fifteen he started to find it difficult to cope with her behaviour. The relationship had become very strained and they were barely talking to one another. Here is a sample of the session when they first discussed Jane's behaviour.

Bob: So what is happening with Jane?

Peter: She is such a problem I don't know what to do with her any more. I feel like giving up. She seems to take pride in not doing what I want and being difficult.

Bob: That must be hard for you, but do you know what you actually want her to do differently?

Peter: I don't know – act her age, stop deliberately infuriating me by being on the phone the whole time, clean up her room . . .

Bob: So one thing you want her to do is clean up her room – and keep it tidy?

Peter: Yes, but she will never do that!

Bob: OK, but instead of focusing on what she will not do let's focus for a moment on what you want. Give me one more positive thing you want her to do. We can deal later with how realistic it is.

Peter: Well, I would like her to tell me what time she is coming in.

Bob: Great – now you are looking at what you want. What else about her behaviour do you want to change?

Peter: Well . . .

Eventually Peter was able to describe how he wanted Jane to behave rather than how difficult she was or what he did not want her to do.

Peter's reaction when Bob asked him to focus on what he wanted rather than how difficult the situation was is very typical. When we have become exasperated with an individual or a situation, it is very human to keep emphasising how bad the situation is and how frustrated we feel. But by focusing on the negatives we keep the situation frozen in the problem state. This leads us to react to them in the same way each time, which gets the same response. We then become more frustrated and the vicious circle goes on.

We can stop the circle by looking at what we do want rather than what we don't want. Once we know what we want we can establish how far we have to go to get there. Then it becomes easier to determine what is stopping change occurring.

With Peter, for instance, we looked at each of the areas that he had identified. We concentrated on facts rather than opinions. We found that Jane only cleared up her room about once every six months and did the washing up about once a week. Once we had established a baseline we could look at what was stopping Peter bringing about the behaviour changes he wanted and then plan for improvement.

Once Peter began to try out some of the ideas we developed, Jane did not suddenly start behaving like a well-balanced adult (this is the real world, after all!). However, because he was now focusing on what he wanted, he did not concentrate so much on Jane's faults, and her behaviour started to improve.

So, in GROW terms, the problem that Peter was facing was that he had a Goal to see changes in his daughter's behaviour, and the Obstacle that she was not changing in the way he wanted her to. It was not that she was a 'bad' person or that she did not care about what he wanted, but a pattern had been established which neither person could change.

A problem always has two parts

In GROW terms, a problem always has two parts. First there is the Goal, something we are trying to accomplish. Second, there is the Obstacle: something opposing and blocking it, which appears to prevent us from doing or achieving what we want. So when we talk about a problem in GROW, what we mean is that we are trying to accomplish something but we are being obstructed in some way.

To illustrate this, let's say you have to be at an important meeting in half an hour, your car has broken down and there is no alternative form of transport. In this case getting to the meeting is your Goal and the lack of transport is the Obstacle, and you have a clear problem. You can now start to plan how to get around the Obstacle.

There was a 'problem' element to most of the Goals that our Test Team members had set. The issue was that they did not know how to achieve their Goal, that they had not defined it clearly or that there seemed to be insurmountable blocks to moving forward.

In order to solve a problem you have to be clear on the elements that make it up. If any of the elements are not clear or are ill defined then the problem will be very hard to solve. This lack of clarity caused a lot of the frustration that our Test Team members had experienced in their previous attempts to achieve their Goals.

With a project, on the other hand, to make progress might take effort and time but we know how we are going to accomplish it, or we are confident we can overcome any Obstacles that arise. So there is nothing really stopping us moving forward.

The power of GROW with problems

Part of the power of the GROW process is that it automatically turns problems into projects. Once we have defined where we are, where we want to go and what is stopping us moving from one point to another, we have already defined the elements of our 'problem'. With these clearly and accurately identified, it is comparatively straightforward to find ways around the Obstacles.

Susan's Goal was to learn Dutch to a certain level. When she started working through the stages of the GROW process, she wrote to us:

> I am a perfectionist. This seems to affect people in one of two ways. It either drives them on to higher and greater things for fear of not being good enough, or the fear of making mistakes paralyses them into doing only the simplest and safest of tasks, procrastinating and giving up at the first hurdle when anything a little more challenging looms. I fall into the second camp.
>
> This was why it was such a revelation to me to separate the Goal from the Obstacles. This frees me up to dream. I am now realising how this overwhelm/panic/give-up-and-run-away pattern runs through every area of my life, big things and very small things. I can't do my GROW home-work, can't de-clutter my house, can't take over our business, can't get back to the world of work, can't improve my kids' eating habits, can't get fit, etc., and it's making me miserable. Everything seems to be too much; I am overwhelmed and never tackle anything of importance at all.

Once Susan learned to separate out the elements of the problem she was less 'paralysed' by her perfectionism and able to take issues one at a time. Many of us would share some of Susan's feeling of being overwhelmed, that 'it is all too much so I can't face doing anything'. That powerful feeling had kept her at home for two years, not able to move back into the world after the birth of her children. Not addressing our problems in an effective way has very real costs attached.

Many of our Test Team members commented on how the

GROW process enabled them to deal with issues that had been troubling them for years, and we were delighted that this simple and elegant methodology had such a powerful effect on their lives.

In saying this we are not denying the real Obstacles some people have when attempting to achieve significant Goals, but until you look at the problem in a structured way it is very hard to assess what the real Obstacles are and to address them effectively.

There is something very human about wanting to justify where we are and why we cannot get what we want. We found well over half our Test Team brought up their Obstacles before they had even clearly defined their Goal. Michelle expressed it well when she said, 'Breaking the process down into small components makes it all more achievable. Rather than just feeling "Oh my God, I am never going to accomplish that", I feel there is something I can do.'

In Chapter 8, on Obstacles, we cover the difference between a justification and a real Obstacle so that you can decide for yourself whether your Obstacles are really stopping you moving forward.

We have now looked at the various types of Goals you can create around doing, having, being and making decisions. We have also explained the difference between a problem and a project and how to create a powerful defining moment. In the next chapter we help you choose a particular topic for the Goal you are going to work with using the GROW process.

6

Creating your
Goal statement

The elements of an effective Goal statement
Choosing your Goal
Creating a defining moment
Writing your Goal statement
Auditing your Goal statement

Reading tips
Test your Goal thoroughly.
Avoid compromise.
Take a risk.
Be brave.

'It's a goal!' The ball thuds into the back of the net, the crowd rises and half the players hug each other in a frenzy. When considering our personal Goals, there is a lot we can learn from their equivalent on the football pitch.

The scoring of goals is the sole purpose of a game of football. They are the difference between victory and defeat, promotion and relegation, and lots more. Goals are the defining moments of the game: you either score them or you don't, and no one, player or supporter, is in any doubt what they look, feel and sound like when they occur. In this chapter, we encourage you to consider and visualise your Goal in the same unambiguous way.

Take a few moments now to imagine a football team on the pitch playing their hearts out and scoring that essential goal. Picture the scene, hear the cheers, feel the energy and get in touch with the emotions. If the image of a football team does not work for you, use something similar.

ASK YOURSELF

What can I learn from this experience that could be relevant for the setting and getting of my personal Goals?

Here are some of the similarities which have occurred to us:

- When the teams are playing, their main focus is on scoring in the opposition's goal. All their intention is directed towards these unmistakable targets. You need a similar centre of attention to achieve your Goal.

- Motivation is often the only thing which separates the winning team from the losers. That is why we have called this book *Grow Your Own Carrot*. However, maintaining motivation, particularly when things might not be going so well, is not always easy.

- Strategy plays a huge part in the game of football and also in the game of life. That is why using a process like GROW to define and score your Goals is so important. Before a match the teams have a game plan. We help you create one, too. The strategy also usually involves an intensive study of the competition, how they play and how they can be defeated.

With our personal Goals the competition is usually easy to identify – just look in the mirror! Unfortunately, we are capable of sabotaging ourselves without any interference from others, although other people can threaten our Goal-scoring ability too.

- The best teams believe without a shadow of a doubt that they *are* the best team. And guess what? They perform like the best team too. While we understand this intellectually, limiting beliefs inevitably build up over the years which sabotage our efforts and are hard to shift. These can include beliefs that we are not good enough, that it is others who achieve their dreams, that we are too old or not sufficiently capable. We are here to help you challenge those beliefs so you are free to achieve your Goals without your mind holding you back.

- The scoring of goals has a massive impact on team and supporter morale. It is just the same with achieving the things you want in your life. The sense of satisfaction when you score a Goal can be huge, and when you have achieved one Goal lots of others can fall into place quite naturally. You can even learn a lot from losing – to help you win next time.

- It takes a lot of skill to become the kind of football player who scores goals time and time again. That is why football teams practise virtually every day. As you use the GROW process, you will need to gain knowledge and practise new skills to achieve your Goals. The good news is that, once you've learnt them, they become second nature and increase your capabilities.

- Finally, with every goal comes a celebration, and we place a lot of emphasis on ensuring that you celebrate not when you reach your ultimate Goal but as you complete the steps along the way. Often in football the goals scored in a match are shown as edited highlights. In just the same way, achieving personal Goals through this book will be highlights of your life.

The elements of a effective Goal statement

Timing

In the GROW Test Team project we set a time span of eight weeks for participants to achieve their Goals. This seemed a reasonable period to accomplish something worthwhile and to keep everyone together as we worked through the process. For many, the eight weeks worked out just fine. However, different Goals required different time scales. Some participants achieved their Goal well within the eight-week period and even started another, while others were still going strong when we held the closing celebration party. Deciding how long you will take to achieve your Goal is an obvious but very important step. We would suggest that a period of eight weeks is the maximum you should go for.

You may have a major Goal that you want to accomplish which cannot be completed in eight weeks. In that case, break the Goal down into a sub Goal that you could conclude within a reasonable period of time. For instance, if you want to entirely change your career, a sub Goal could be 'To have an interview for a job that I really want to do by the end of eight weeks'. If you do not know what alternative career you want, your Goal might be 'To have three alternative career directions which appeal to me and have a plan for how I am going to investigate each one by the end of eight weeks'.

Taking just an element of the Goal can really help clarify your objective. This is known as 'chunking down'. Learning Dutch could be a lifetime's work, but a first step might be to take a beginner's Dutch course. A more interesting Goal would be taking your partner out to dinner in three months and ordering in Dutch. How large you make your Goal will depend on how close you are to it at the moment. We look at this aspect in Chapter 7, 'Creating your Reality statement'.

Ray's original Goal was 'To be happy with myself'. The issue with big 'global' Goals like this is that it is very difficult to know when you have achieved them, and then the Goal as stated implies that you stay happy for ever.

The Goal itself was certainly something Ray aspired to. He was learning to live by himself again after a couple of unsuccessful relationships and was unhappy about his social life. He deeply disliked spending any time alone. You might think that this is a pretty low-level Goal, but for Ray it was a serious challenge. We worked with him on narrowing the Goal to find a 'chunk' that he could accomplish in eight weeks. After we discussed it with him, he revised his Goal to 'Spend a weekend by myself doing things I enjoy and being happy'. We agreed that this was something he could realistically achieve in eight weeks.

ASK YOURSELF

Can I really achieve this Goal in the time I have allocated?

It is better to be realistic on timing at the outset than to find you are over-stretching yourself.

Making it measurable

A Goal needs to be as specific and measurable as possible. Compare 'Becoming a fitter person' to 'Being able to run twice around the track in Battersea Park in 10 minutes'. The first statement is vague, while the second is measurable and could be easily verified. The key to setting clear Goals is to check whether you can imagine watching it on a film. If you can picture the actual scene, then the Goal will be clear.

Being precise

It is important to be precise when stating your Goal. As Chris's old sales manager from the 1970s used to say, in his gruff East London accent, when salespeople were waffling about whether they had got an order: 'You can't be half pregnant!' So 'To halve my credit card debt in six weeks' is pretty clear, as is 'To lose 12 pounds in six weeks'. However, there are some traps to avoid when setting factual Goals.

'To get at least three job offers' sounds fine, but on further consideration we can see that by saying 'at least' the actual point at which the Goal is scored is unclear. It is clearer to give the number you want and use that as your Goal. Of course, you might like five job offers, but if the Goal is three you will know that when the third one comes in you will have achieved the Goal.

Being positive

A Goal can be stated in the positive or the negative and, not surprisingly, the positive works best. For example, a being Goal about confidence could be stated in the negative as 'to be less shy' or in the positive as 'to be more confident'. Of course, we need the Goal to be stated more specifically, but 'to be less shy' focuses on the original problem. There is intent to reduce something, but it is still negative. Being more confident starts you thinking what the *positive* would look like. It is far easier to envisage situations where you are more confident than ones where you are less shy.

It is surprising how we can weaken our aspirations with negative language. It is as if the negative has such a hold that we cannot even envisage the positive side. It is interesting that when we talk about diet we always refer to weight loss rather than what we gain by being slimmer. If we reframe the Goal in terms of what we will gain rather than what we will lose, the motivation will be stronger.

A shift to the positive can be very moving. Carrie's Goal was to change her relationship with her son. Her original Goal statement was 'To spend an evening with my son when he does not once say, "Mum, you don't understand" '. A more positive alternative was 'Spending an evening together where he says, "Mum, you are great!" '. That was what she really wanted to hear, and she was far more motivated to achieve it.

Choosing your Goal

Goals are about you taking control of your life, rather than life controlling you. They are the difference between guiding the ship to a specific shore and being buffeted by the winds to 'who knows where'.

ASK YOURSELF

Have I largely been in control of my life or has my life been in control of me?

Take a few moments to think back on your life and some of the jobs you have had, your relationships, the places you have been to, the things you have learnt and accomplished.

If you are like most people, then many of these things just came about by chance. You happened to be looking in the paper; a friend suggested something; you were in the right place at the right time – or maybe the wrong one. The outcomes might have been good or bad, but the point is you did not specifically choose them.

With Goals, on the other hand, you get to choose. You are in the driving seat, not just admiring the view. If you are afraid of making a change then it might help to remember that life is changing all the time, whether we want it or not. Why not take control and make some changes that you really want?

'The amazing thing about the GROW process is that you can achieve almost anything you really want, but you have to choose whether to give it energy or not,' Molly said. She had discovered that she could use the GROW process to take charge of her own life. However, once we know that we *can* change, it follows that we have the responsibility to make the changes if we are not happy with our lives. Being helpless is in some respects easier.

You have now hopefully decided on a Goal you are going for. It would be helpful to write down your Goal now, before reading any more of this chapter. It does not matter if it is not very well defined yet. A vague Goal is fine at this stage.

Outline Goal

My Goal at this point in the process is

Great! Now you have articulated your Goal we are going to show you how to turn it into a very specific Goal statement. This is where your Goal gets crystallised into the essence of what you want to achieve. After you have completed this process it should be clear to anyone who reads it precisely what you aim to achieve and by when. As you read the following pages it is a good idea to keep checking back on your Goal to see if any of the points we are making relate to your Goal, and change it accordingly. We give you a final opportunity to do this at the end of the chapter, before we ask you to commit to the Goal statement you will use for the rest of this book.

Quick fix or lasting change?

As well as achieving a quick visible result, a Goal can offer you an opportunity to make a more lasting change. Lisa's Goal was to lose weight. It is relatively easy, although possibly dangerous, to lose weight by suddenly reducing food intake. Lisa realised that her eating habits also needed changing. Adopting a more healthy diet meant she could not only achieve her immediate weight loss target but also establish an eating pattern which would benefit her after her immediate weight loss target had been achieved. This longer-term gain will apply to any behavioural change, such as being calmer, more organised or less controlling.

Further, higher, faster

A good question to ask when clarifying your Goal is how much of a stretch it would be for you to achieve it. There are two reasons for this question. First, you could be someone who sets very demanding Goals but lacks the drive and determination to see them through to a conclusion. This can also be a way of never achieving anything by making sure the Goal is safely out of sight. A good strategy would be to chunk it down to a manageable size or set a series of milestones which you can reach one after the other.

Alternatively, you might set your ambitions so low that your Goal lacks challenge. The timid 'better not risk it' approach does not serve you well, and we know you are capable of far more. We can say this for sure, without even knowing you, as we are all capable of far more than we allow ourselves. That is why, when people achieve something, they often say that they surprised themselves. Try the following Discovery Exercise, which comes from *Centred Skier* by Denise McCluggage.

Discovery Exercise 1: Unused potential

Objective: To use a physical exercise to demonstrate how much of your potential you currently use and have available

1 Stand with your right hand held straight in front of you at about shoulder height. Now turn your body along with your arm, as you sweep it to the right as far as you can go without moving your feet or bending your knees or waist. Make sure you turn as far as you can. Sighting along your finger, make a visual benchmark on the wall to notice how far you have turned.

2 Now unwind to where you started. Rest your arm for a moment. Then do the rotation again, this time noticing where your eyeballs are as you turn. Chances are, they are in the far right corner of their sockets – leading the way for your head, shoulders and hips as you turn.

3 Come back and start again. Lower your arms for a moment, then make the turn again, only this time direct your eyes to the left-hand side of your sockets as you turn to the right. This may feel difficult at first. Do the rotation with your eyes in the left-hand side of your sockets and turning to the right five times. Lower your arm between rotations.

4 Then do another series of rotations, this time leaving your hips behind, i.e. twisting them towards the left as you turn the rest of your body to the right. It will not look pretty, but that is not the point! Do this five times.

5 After you have done all this, go back and turn to the right exactly as you did the first time. Twist your eyes, head and body along with your arm. Now note where your finger is in relation to the first benchmark on the wall. If the instructions have been clear, your new mark will be distinctly further round than your first one.

You might think that this is simply a physical trick and bears no relation to Goal-setting. Well, it is certainly a physical exercise, but what you have proved, if the exercise worked for you, is that the point where you thought you had to stop could be easily expanded by some simple exercises. There was potential to go much further than you first realised.

The same principle that applies to our bodies also applies to our minds. Our capacity to achieve Goals is much greater than we generally believe. As you work through this book, we will show you exercises to develop your potential and expand your Goal-achieving capacity.

Is there a sub Goal?

Sometimes gaining a Goal can involve sub Goals which need to be achieved in order to reach your overall objective. These are not just actions to support your Goal but something which is a whole undertaking in itself. Charles was a computer consultant in his thirties, whose Goal was to create two offers of employment. In considering his Goal, he realised that to give himself the best chance in the interview process he needed to increase his confidence and, more specifically, how he presented and sold himself in an interview.

Being more competent in an interview situation is a sub Goal which has a number of elements, including developing answers and improving his approach and skill.

Donald's Goal was originally to find a new career. He had been a financial advisor for many years and knew he wanted to find an alternative career that appealed more to his values. We asked him what he could achieve in eight weeks towards his Goal. He was not sure he could achieve a new career in the time, so he decided to identify and participate in ten creative activities that would help him to choose the direction he could take in order to change career. With this Goal he could explore the creative directions that interested him and be sure he had accomplished his Goal.

Sub Goals can occur at any stage in the GROW process and often involve acquiring new skills or knowledge which are required to progress your Goal.

Value and benefit

There is little point in going through the process of achieving a Goal if you are not going to obtain some definable value or benefit from it. There has to be something in it for you and maybe also for those around you. In considering this, it is important that you understand the value the Goal gives you. It might not be obvious to others. For example, sometimes new-comers to his meditation group ask Chris why he opens his house twice a month to give free meditation sessions. They find this extraordinary, but for him the experience of gathering together a community of stillness is sublime and beyond price.

ASK YOURSELF

What would be the real benefit for me and others if I achieved this Goal?

When you feel you have a satisfactory answer, ask the question again of that answer. You can repeat this until you feel you have got down to the core value of having your Goal.

Here is an example of the process. Chris asked Carol the value questions around her Goal, which was to get her diploma in mental healthcare.

Chris: What benefit or value would getting your diploma in mental healthcare give you?

Carol: It would prove that I am able to do something.

Chris: And what would proving you were able to do something do for you?

Carol: It would make me feel taller.

Chris: And what would feeling taller give you?

Carol: It would give me the strength to stand up for myself.

Chris: And what would the strength to stand up for yourself give you?

Carol: It would give me confidence.

An interesting sequence also occurred when she was asked about the value of achieving another Goal, which was to lose 11 pounds.

Chris: What would losing 11 pounds give you?

Carol: It would make me feel proud of myself.

Chris: What value or benefit would feeling proud of yourself give you?

Carol: It would make me feel sexier.

Chris: And what value or benefit would feeling sexier give you?

Carol: It would give me more confidence.

So two very different Goals can lead you to the same core value. This is very useful information, because once you know your core values you can develop other Goals which are in line with them.

ASK YOURSELF

Is there an alternative Goal which would satisfy the same core value as my original Goal?

If you come up with a number of Goals in answer to this question, you now have a choice as to which of the Goals you wish to go for.

Creating a defining moment

The stronger you make your Goal in your mind, the greater the possibility you will get to see that Goal achieved in your Reality. This is fundamental, not cosmetic. The idea of a defining moment is not only to visualise but also plan an event around the precise time and situation when your Goal will be achieved, and incorporate this into your Goal statement.

In creating a defining moment, the key question is: what is the precise moment when you will know you have achieved your Goal? What will be happening? How will it look and feel, what will you hear or maybe even taste or smell? With some Goals, like getting married or a job offer, the event is contained in the process. You get a job offer in the post or you say, 'I do'.

When you are setting a Goal it is very important to have a point in time where you know you have definitely achieved your objective. While in some instances it may be very clear that the Goal has been reached, in many instances it is not. If you have a clear time when you know the Goal is achieved, it gives you a 'laser point' to aim for and avoids any ambiguity.

Some people have difficulty creating a defining moment due to fear of failure. By making an event out of achieving the Goal, inviting friends and so on, you are really committed, so far more is resting on your success. This will be true even if the actual Goal remains the same. So what will be exciting and motivational for some could be hugely fearful for others.

ASK YOURSELF

Would I rather increase the sense of achievement in gaining my Goal or worry about not making it?

Here is how to create clear defining moments for different types of Goals.

A defining moment for a decision Goal

Making a decision can be hard, and some decisions just never get made at all. The secret is to have a clear defining moment for the point of decision which is compelling and final. Once you have established this you know you are committed to making a decision, and it is relatively straightforward to use the GROW process to steadily work towards it.

If at all possible, you should include in the defining moment how you will deal with any unfinished business relating to the Options you did not choose. In this way we are turning the *defining moment* into a *deciding moment*.

Let us take an example which most of us have faced in our lives: deciding whether to stay or leave a spouse or partner. Remember, we are not concerned here with the very real issues associated with such a decision. We are setting up the Goal in such a way that a decision is unavoidable, and these issues can then be examined in the light of that event.

Without a decision in a relationship situation you might well be living a sort of uncommitted half-life, not experiencing the joy of a really fulfilling relationship and not free to create another. If this does not apply to you, don't worry; it is an example which can be applied to any decision, large or small.

For example, Sara felt that her relationship with her

boyfriend was not really going anywhere, and to move it forward would involve one or other of them relocating to another country. She also had a number of other concerns about the relationship although he was a 'really nice guy'.

We agreed that her Goal would be 'I will do everything required to make a decision regarding my future life. To confirm this, I will book a table for two at a nice restaurant for Saturday 27 March. I will invite my boyfriend to acknowledge how much I love him and start planning our life together, or I will invite my best friend for her to witness the new single me and plan what support I will need to live that life, part of which will involve telling my boyfriend of my decision.'

In this Goal she has included what she needs to do to inform her partner of her decision. As a deciding moment we could also have focused on the geographical issue and made the Goal about visiting a travel agent to arrange her travel to join her boyfriend, with the alternative of arranging a holiday on her own or with a close friend.

You may well be reading this thinking, 'Wow, that's a bit harsh!' Well, yes, maybe, but in forcing the issue you make it crunch time. Also bear in mind that unmade decisions can affect others as well as ourselves. Isn't it fairer for all to be clear about your intentions and what you want for the future, rather than remaining uncommitted and compromising? Anyway, the romantics among you need not fear. Sara invited her boyfriend to a wonderful restaurant in Milan, having decided that she wanted to live her life with him.

There are lots of ways to devise a decision Goal like this, and probably the acid test is how it feels when you have articulated it. If you get that 'this is it!' feeling in the pit of your stomach, with some fear mixed in with the excitement, then you have probably picked the defining moment which will work for you.

If, on the other hand, the defining moment does not touch you emotionally, then it will probably not help you arrive at a decision and you will lose interest. There is always a danger of 'chickening out' on a really well-defined 'moment of truth' Goal.

However, the GROW process and the support systems we suggest will help keep you on track.

If you are continually worrying whether you have made the right decision, the energy you waste will slow your progress on your chosen path. That is why you need to gather as much information as possible before making the decision, and here the Obstacles and Options stages of the GROW process really come into their own.

If you can identify as many Obstacles and Options as possible and have a good process for weighing them up, you will, as the saying goes, 'have covered all your options'. You should also have some good reasons why some are better than others. In Chapter 11, 'The Way Forward', we will show you how to do this simply and effectively.

Defining moments for other types of Goal

At the point when you achieve your Goal there should be a moment when you know you have achieved it. For a weight loss Goal, it could be stepping on the scales at the gym. If it is to have an article published, it might be buying the magazine and reading your words. The key to creating a good defining moment is that when the moment happens there should be no doubt that the Goal is achieved. It is also useful to include a degree of celebration which can mark your success.

Here are some Goal examples with an appropriate defining moment.

Goal	Defining moment
To leave a job	Handing in your resignation to your boss
To move house	Accepting an offer on your existing house or signing the purchase agreement for a new one

To move country	Receiving your acceptance notification from the country you wish to move to or buying your travel ticket
To start a course of some kind	Signing the enrolment form or paying the fee
To redesign a room	Inviting friends around for a celebratory dinner when the work is finished
To get married	When you say 'I do'

Here is a real defining moment example from the Test Team.

Nicole wanted her products displayed in ten leading Belgian stores within eight weeks. This was excellent in terms of measurability. We had a timescale and the number of stores; she knew what her products were and which shops she wanted to target. This was good, but could be made even better.

Products in shops are very visible. They are either there or not. It should be possible in a day to go and see them. While you are about it, why not make it a real occasion? Nicole had some good friends who were supporting her, so maybe one or more of them could be included, too. Her day might start with a champagne breakfast with her friend in a nice Brussels hotel. They could set off in a beautifully polished car or even hire a chauffeur. (OK, maybe we are getting carried away here!) At each shop they could take a picture of the products on display and perhaps have a little 'thank you' present for the manager. A nice lunch, the last of the viewings and back home at the end of an unforgettable day. The pictures might go into an album or be put together in a collage for her office wall to demonstrate her success and encourage more.

This is more exciting than a few products piled on shelves or some order forms in her hand. It is even possible to plan the event now, invite the friends, book the breakfast and hire the chauffeur. Now all Nicole has to do is sell the products to complete the picture.

Nicole's Goal became 'to take my friend on an exciting fun-filled day to see my products displayed in ten leading Belgian stores'. This is a defining moment which is really worth staying focused and motivated for. In the Way Forward stage of the GROW process you will see how to plan that defining moment so it really lives up to your mental picture. In this way we are not only turning our dreams into reality but making our Reality into a dream.

You might not visualise an event like Nicole's, but a more private moment. It could be seeing the first page of your book on the computer screen, stepping on your scales at 10.00 a. m. on 28 March and seeing them register 140 pounds, or the feeling of setting foot on the dance floor as the salsa music starts to play.

Achieving a worthwhile Goal is hard work and there are likely to be a number of issues along the way. But by making your Goal into a defining moment you give it real impact and you are far more likely to stay motivated and engaged. You will also have a truly fulfilling and memorable experience when you finally achieve your objective, and let's be honest – you deserve it. The bigger and brighter you can make your Goal, the better. The more you can visualise your Goal and make it exciting, the more you will stay motivated to turn that image into reality.

Discovery Exercise 2: Picture your Goal

Objective: To sense the experience of your Goal being achieved

ASK YOURSELF

Imagine the moment when you know you have achieved your Goal. Imagine what it would feel like to achieve your

---

Goal. See a mental picture of how you will look when you get there. Hear what you and others will say when you have achieved this. You may even be able to smell and taste something. If your Goal was to learn bakery then that would certainly be the case!

My Goal looks like	
My Goal feels like	
My Goal sounds like	
My Goal smells like	
My Goal tastes like	
Now tick which sense was the strongest for you	✓

For example, when Carol pictured the moment of when she achieved her Goal of losing 11 pounds she saw fireworks, jumped up and down and felt taller and lighter in her chest. She heard herself cry out for joy. What a wonderful sensation to look forward to as she munched her way through her crisp-breads!

There are a number of reasons why sensing your Goal before you achieve it is important. By visualising the Goal as clearly as you can, you can experience whether it will really give you what you want. You might well feel yourself getting hotter or your lips starting to form a smile. This is the 'warm soup glow' of a worthwhile Goal. If you have it then it is a sure sign that this Goal is for you. As you push on with the GROW process you can recreate this experience any time you want, to remind yourself why you are making all this effort. Start with the sense which was strongest for you, the one you ticked in the exercise.

If you find this visualisation exercise hard, then maybe it is not a Goal you can really identify with in any way. You do not have to know exactly what this future experience will be like. When you get there it might feel totally different. For example, your Goal might be to go up in a hot air balloon, and at this moment you might have no idea how that would look and feel. As long as the idea appeals to you now, that is fine, even if when you get up in the air the sensation is nothing like you imagined.

In a teleclass Andrew was discussing his Goal to start a football academy linked to a full-time football club. We asked him, 'Do you think this is something that you think you can achieve in eight weeks?' He thought about it and replied that getting the whole thing up and running was not feasible in eight weeks. We then asked, 'If we were from Mars and came to see you, how would we know that you had achieved something?' He replied, 'If we had the first game in the club strip I would know I had really made progress.' It was clear from the tone of his voice that he could see his players going out on the field for that first game in their club strip and could feel what seeing that would be like for him.

Writing your Goal statement

Watch those verbs

'Find', 'identify', 'develop' all sound like good words to have in a Goal, as they indicate a process, but in fact they are quite unspecific. It will not necessarily be clear when we have found, identified or developed what we want. It is more effective to use verbs which by their very nature demonstrate the act of accomplishment. For instance, to sign something is pretty definite, so is embarking, seeing, buying or enrolling. They are focused on an instant, not a process.

Loss and gain

It is important to look at not only what you will gain when you achieve your Goal but what you could lose as well. Leaving something behind is an intrinsic part of any change, and this is an aspect of achievement we often do not consider. Maybe what we lose is purely negative, so it does not matter, but we can lose positive aspects as well. For instance, we might lose a sense of security if we are thinking about changing a boring job into one which is more interesting but with less certainty.

Several Test Team participants commented that using GROW meant that they had to take responsibility for their situation and give up not being responsible and blaming others. Lindsey was trying to get her spending under control. She was finding it difficult to get to grips with the facts and wrote to us, 'I have always enjoyed being a bit of a defiant rebel – being aware about what I am spending means that I have to give up that part of me.'

ASK YOURSELF

What will I lose as well as gain if I achieve my Goal?
Is there anything I have to make provision for along the way?

Be realistic

If you start out believing your Goal is going to be difficult then you will be dead right! By defining your future experience in this way you are virtually guaranteeing a hard time. On the other hand, thinking the Goal will be easy when in fact it is quite a stretch is likely to result in you having a serious loss of confidence at some stage in the process. So when choosing your Goal, be realistic about the extent of the challenge. You have to work in the area of the possible, and this is particularly true of the first Goal you set using the GROW process. We want you to prove the process, not necessarily how tough you are, although of course a personal fitness target could be your Goal.

For your initial attempt at the GROW process select a Goal which is both a bit out of your reach and something you really want. That will give you the best chance of success.

Your Goal statement

Having read this chapter you can hopefully now see a number of ways you can create a specific Goal statement which is:

- motivational;
- measurable;
- believable.

So now have a go at creating your own 'draft' Goal statement.

My 'draft' Goal statement

Auditing your Goal statement

Having drafted your Goal statement, here is a checklist you can use to see if it fulfils all the criteria we have set out in this chapter. Now you have your support group or buddy in place (you have, haven't you?) use them to validate your Goal. Send them the checklist and your draft Goal and see if they agree you have something which they can support. It is important that you include a moment when they will know you have achieved your Goal and how you will celebrate with them.

Discovery Exercise 3: Goal statement checklist

Objective: To ensure your Goal is stated and understood in a way which will really work for you

Use the following questions to check that your Goal meets the requirements you have read in this chapter. If you get a 'no' for any question then it is a good idea to go back and consider revising it. Also ask your supporters or buddy to check your Goal against the list and see what they say. They should be objective and tell you what you need to hear with no fudging. Everyone should understand the Goal immediately with no further explanation from you.

Is my Goal a manageable size and not so big that it overwhelms me?
Is my Goal largely within my competence and control?
Is my Goal measurable?
Is my Goal stated in the positive?
Does my Goal have a clear time line with a completion date?
Is there a clear defining moment when I will know I have succeeded?
Is the Goal realistic?
Is the Goal something I want rather than something that I feel I should do?
Is the Goal significant for me?
Do I know clearly the benefits I will get out of achieving this Goal?
Do I know what I will lose if I do not get my Goal?
How would I feel about that?
Do I feel motivated and inspired by my Goal?

Is this a real Goal I want to go for or would I prefer it as a dream?
Have I really asked for what I want or am I settling for something less?
Have I thought about any risks (financial, physical, personal or emotional) that I might face in achieving this Goal?
Does my Goal conflict with any other Goals or aspirations I have?
Have I included some point of celebration?

OK, now is the time to commit. It is essential that you do this before reading any more of this book, as everything which follows will relate to the Goal you have set.

My Goal commitment
The specific and measurable Goal I will achieve using the GROW process is
I will achieve it by (*time scale*)
I will have achieved it when (*defining moment*)
This Goal is important for me because (*value of Goal*)
This time the experience will be different because (*complete only if you have ever previously tried to make changes in this area of your life and failed*)

> To achieve this Goal I will use the following values and personal resources
>
> ---
>
> Signed
> Dated

If you are still reading and have not yet signed your Goal statement,

---

ASK YOURSELF

What could be preventing me from taking this step?

Remember, we said this is a book for action, not just for interest, and we really want you in action. Maybe you need to share where you are with your support group or buddy.

If you have filled out and signed the completion form above, then we really want to acknowledge your efforts in getting to this point on the path to success. Setting a clear direction by stating your Goal in this way is *the* most important step in the GROW process.

Now we know what you want to achieve, all we have to do is get you there. You have shown strong intent so far and we can ask for nothing more. Maybe this is a time for a 'mini celebration' to acknowledge your accomplishment. Give yourself a treat. We look forward to helping you achieve your Goal in the following chapters.

7

Creating your
Reality statement

Reading tips
See the Goal from start to finish.
Be practical.
Stay positive.
Have patience.
Be realistic.

What is Reality?

If you have been following the GROW process so far, you will
have created a clear Goal statement, and for the moment we

are going to leave it just over the horizon. We now want to bring your attention to where you stand right now in terms of your Goal. This is your current Reality.

In GROW terms, Reality is neither *good* nor *bad*. Many people find this quite a difficult concept to grasp. When we find ourselves a long way from our Goal and we would like to be closer, it is tempting to label the current situation as bad or wrong. But giving a negative label to a Reality statement is not helpful. It shifts your attention on to the Obstacles before you have a clear idea of where you are right now in the process. It is like a downhill skier racing through trees and focusing only on the trees rather than the gaps between them. The result tends to be a collision with an Obstacle.

Reality versus realistic

The Reality stage of the GROW process can be confusing and is often misunderstood. For example, some participants in the Test Team thought creating their Reality statement was the same as being realistic about the chance that they would achieve their Goal, but that is not the case.

Here is an example from a teleclass.

Lauren was trying hard to define her Reality statement. Her Goal was to meet five guys who shared her values (we had already defined what these were) and to go on a date with one of them. She had correctly identified how far she had got towards her Goal, but in the middle of the conversation she suddenly exclaimed, 'It is really hard to look at it in this way because I don't know when I am going to be able to spend any time on it.'

Lauren had fallen into the trap of thinking that Reality was the same as realistic. She was an IT project manager and had got into the habit of working long hours and putting her own needs second. Even though she had set the Goal and it was something she really wanted, she could not see how it was going to be realistic to achieve it. Because she was anxious about whether she could achieve her Goal with the way her life was set up at the moment, she was jumping ahead in her process.

We asked Lauren to consider whether she was jumping ahead to Obstacles rather than looking at where she was currently in terms of her Goal. She thought about it for a second and said, 'I guess I am.'

There is nothing wrong with identifying Obstacles at this stage – please keep a note of them, as they will be dealt with in the next chapter.

What is a Reality statement?

In order to create a Reality statement correctly, it is important to identify all the steps in the process to complete your Goal from start to finish. You then need to record accurately how many of the steps you have completed. If you know that there are ten steps to achieve your Goal and you have completed three of them, then your Reality statement is that you are on Step Three. The Reality statement should include the stages you had completed *at the point you set your Goal*. This is a key point, because as soon as you start to move towards your Goal your Reality will change.

Let's take the example of passing a driving test. There are clearly many steps between having the initial impulse to learn to drive and being given your pass certificate. You have to find an instructor, take lessons, practise your skills, learn the Highway Code, rehearse the test, deal with nerves and so on. Your Reality would be how many of these steps you had completed at the point you set the Goal.

Here are some real examples from the Test Team.

Writing a book

Molly was in the process of writing a book. Her initial Goal was simply to assemble the various chapters into a presentable format so she could have the satisfaction of seeing it finished. She had already completed many of the stages. Her Reality statement was that she had a clear story-line in her head and had handwritten a first draft, though there were four chapters missing. This showed exactly how many of the stages she had completed.

Eight weeks later we all took part in her defining moment as she read the first moving chapter at the Test Team celebration party. Interestingly, after Molly had taken this step forward, she started giving the book to more people and the feedback she received gave her the confidence to take another step forward. She is currently negotiating with a well-known publisher to get the book into print.

Producing a DVD

Alan's Goal was 'Finishing a DVD of an event I filmed, to the point where I can send it out to potential buyers'. He looked at all the steps he needed to take from start to finish. His Reality statement was that 'I have viewed all the material and done a first edit'.

Better communication

Carrie's Goal was 'To communicate with my child during an evening in such a way that he says, "Mum, you are really great" '. The Reality statement was 'At the moment he says, "Mum, you really don't understand" to me at least twice every time I speak to him.'

A point for reflection

The Reality statement is an important staging post allowing you to look in both directions: back to what you have already accomplished and forward to what you have yet to do to achieve your Goal. From this vantage point it is quite common to realise that the distance to achieving a Goal is too far in one hop and the Goal should be reduced, or perhaps a sub Goal created. Or indeed the opposite can happen, when you might realise that you are nearer your Goal than you thought you were. That can be simply accepted as great news, or you might want to increase the challenge and extend your Goal a little further. Much will depend on the situation.

Now that you've got the idea, let's get started on developing a Reality statement for your Goal.

Writing your Reality statement

There are three aspects you need to consider.

Facts

Reality by its very nature needs to be factual. That means taking an honest open approach to where you are and including everything which relates to the subject of your Goal.

Some statements of fact are sufficient in themselves. For instance: 'My CV is fully up to date'; 'I have all the timber I need to build the shed'.

Some factual statements need clarifying before they can be used.

Statement	Clarified statement
'I know some recruitment consultants.'	'I have a list of twelve recruitment consultants on my PC.'
'I am overweight.'	'I weigh 160 pounds, which is about 20 pounds more than my recommended weight.'

Here are some other areas of fact which can be included in drawing up a Reality statement.

Relevant area of fact	Example statement
Facts about time	'I have been looking for a job for the last six months.' 'I have been with my boyfriend for two years.'
Facts about previous attempts	'I have tried to clear out my cupboards three times in the last two years.' 'I have made frequent attempts to reduce my weight, without success.'
Facts about how you react when you do not achieve your Goal	'When I have given up on my weight loss Goals in the past I have become very angry with myself, eaten a lot of junk food and put on all the weight I had lost.' 'The last time I failed the exam I sat down and worked out how I could do better.'
Facts about how others respond	'I have tried to diet many times but my husband does not support me.' 'My mother gives me a lot of encouragement.'

This sort of factual information is very useful as it highlights potential Obstacles and Options, which we address in the next chapters.

Here are some excerpts from the Reality statements of fact

that the Test Team identified. It should be very clear how the factual Reality relates to their Goal.

Caroline, our actress, was trying to get a major acting part. Her Reality statement was:

> I have an agent with a good reputation and excellent connections. However, he does not put me up for many acting roles but mainly commercials. I am scared to call people I should talk to, like casting agents.

Lisa, whose Goal was weight loss, said, 'I currently have no idea what I am eating.'

Iris's Goal was 'To take an advanced salsa class in a venue I like where people celebrate life.'

Her Reality statement was:

1   I go dancing now and then on Friday nights, whenever I feel like it and have energy left, in a club where the lessons are not really 'professionally' given and are for beginners.
2   I often do not go because I feel too tired after a week's work and lack energy.
3   I am not very enthusiastic about the crowd I meet there.

We can see how the Reality statement gives 'advance warning' of the Obstacles that have to be addressed if the Goal is to be achieved.

ASK YOURSELF

What are the basic facts of the Reality of my Goal?

It might be helpful to picture yourself as a police constable being called to give a statement in a court of law. As you imagine reading from your notebook, the judge might say, 'Stick to the facts, please, Constable,' and so you do.

> My Reality statements of fact are

Faculties

As well as the facts, your Reality statements should record the faculties, the skills and capabilities you have which you can use to achieve your Goal. Remember, we are looking for your resources and talents stated in the positive, not what you might lack or do poorly. There will be an opportunity to look at them when we come to the Obstacles section of the GROW process, and to resolve them in Options and the Way Forward.

Reality statements of faculty could include:

I am good at woodwork.
I learn languages easily.
I have already shown huge courage.

Here are some of the faculties which the Test Team had in their Realities:

Daniel, whose Goal was to find a girlfriend, wrote, 'I am very good at starting conversations with women in the street and in clubs.'

Jean had a Goal to get a travel article published. She wrote: 'My friends always kept the letters I wrote to them when I was travelling and told me I should write travel articles.'

ASK YOURSELF

What faculties do I have available to assist me in reaching my Goal?

Here you might like to think of an end-of-term school report which lists what you know and can do. However, this time you get to write it, not the teachers, so you can leave out the poor scores.

My Reality statements of faculties are

Feelings

There is another aspect of Reality which is very important as it can be the source of great insights: your Emotional Reality. These are not factual or faculty statements but statements about your feelings as you stand in your current state, immediately prior to moving forward towards completing your Goal. They are not about the Goal itself but the emotions you have inside right now – your internal emotional Reality.

They could include:

My weight embarrasses me.
I am afraid I cannot write well enough to get something published.
I sometimes think I will never find a job I want to do.

Here are some of the feelings Realities which the Test Team had when considering where they currently stood emotionally in relation to their Goals.

Tiffany had a lot of powerful feelings about her Goal of clearing up her flat. She wrote:

1   The piles of papers, books and clothes in my flat are my way of saying that I can't take care of myself and I need someone else to care enough for me.
2   There is no need to make an effort to make a pleasant environment to live in when there is just me there. I do not deserve a nice space.
3   Sorting through the mess and rearranging the stuff in my apartment would mean putting my stamp on the apartment and finally recognising that my ex-partner has gone and that phase of my life is over.
4   I am feeling a lot of resentment towards my flatmate, that he is invading my personal space. I think that leaving my stuff around is a subconscious claiming of territory, branding the apartment as mine.

Charles wanted a job in IT and had been unemployed for a few months. He said: 'I am feeling very negative about my experience and what I have to offer. These feelings make it very hard for me to go out and continue my job search.'

The feelings you have about your current position are very relevant to your Goal and should be recorded.

ASK YOURSELF

What are my emotional realities when I think about my Goal?

To help you get in touch with these feelings you might like to imagine you are sharing your innermost thoughts with your best friend. If you have set up your support group as we suggested, you should have someone who you can do this with. If you do this with someone, make sure that they just witness your thoughts and feelings, rather than denying them or sympathising with them.

My Reality statements of feelings are

Another way to share your feelings and get in touch with every aspect of your Reality is to talk to yourself. There is no one closer to you than you, although this still requires you to be open and honest.

Just talk into a tape recorder or to a video camera. You have probably seen this done on *Big Brother* or *Video Diaries*. This is a good way of getting in touch with your feelings.

Hidden Reality traps

It is not always easy to be clear on where you are in relation to your Goal. Here are three common traps that you can fall into when defining your Reality.

Focusing on being stuck rather than the Reality

Maria's Goal was to identify three alternative jobs that excited and inspired her. Her first Reality statement was:

There are parts of it [my job] I really like, but mostly I hate it. I have no idea and never have had any idea what I would really like to do. I am always asking people what they would really like to do career wise so that I can judge if I am the only one who doesn't know what to do or not. I do not know where to start!

Maria did not know where to start as she was focusing on the problem rather than the actual Reality of her work. In order to get some information which would help her we asked her to think about which parts of the work she enjoyed and which parts she did not. When she did this she was able to rework her Reality statement. This now read:

I enjoy the investigations part of my job, I love having a mystery to solve. I like nothing better than having a pile of papers on my desk which I have to make sense of. I used to work for charities, which I enjoyed because I felt I was doing something useful. The parts I dislike are the weekly collation of statistics and having to deal with demotivated staff.

Once she had defined her Reality more accurately, creating her Obstacles and Options became much easier. She was able to ask for help in identifying potential careers where she could use her investigative skills and soon had some great leads to potential new jobs.

Defining Reality in different terms than your Goal

Having established a clear Goal, it is important that the rest of the GROW process relates directly to that Goal and not something else. Gabrielle had a Goal to be mentally and physically ready for a major operation. She knew what she meant by 'ready' which was:

- to be able to reach the stairs of my office breathing normally;
- to have control over my voice and breathing at a presentation I have to do before the operation;
- to be calm and relaxed and breathing normally with a normal heart rate by the day of the operation;
- to have lost at least 7 pounds by the time of the operation.

Her initial Reality statement was:

I have set the date for the surgery (13 April) and talked through the technical details with my surgeon and GP. I have set up an action plan (eat at least one fruit a day, ban chocolate and exercise three times for 20 minutes per week). I have started a journal to keep track of my action plan. I have set up a support group to help me with this (the surgeon, my sister, a friend, my buddy). This network of moral and practical support and social control helps me to focus on what I should be doing to achieve my Goal.

These were good ideas in terms of the actions she could take to support herself, but did not tell us how far she was on the way to her Goal at the start of the GROW process. We worked with Gabrielle to define her Reality in terms of her breathing on the stairs currently, heart rate, levels of relaxation and weight. Once she had established these, she could plan to work on the Obstacles and create a Way Forward action plan that took account of what might stop her achieving her Goal.

Listing opinions and beliefs rather than facts

A number of the Test Team had Goals around losing weight. When they came to the Reality section many of them included statements like 'I have no self-discipline.' Of course, lack of discipline may be relevant to their attempts at weight loss. However, when identifying our Reality in the GROW process we are looking for simple statements of fact rather than personal criticism.

The statement 'I have no self-discipline' does not say anything about the Reality about weight loss at the point when the Goal was started. If the statement read 'I often keep a packet of biscuits on my desk and eat them unconsciously', that would provide good information about the current situation and enable you to plan change. Opinions and beliefs generally do not help the process and tend to cause confusion further on in the process.

The danger in the Reality section is that the frustration we have at the current situation takes over and prevents clear thinking. It is really worth taking the time to record all the facts separated from Obstacles, opinions and beliefs. With these correctly identified in relation to our Goal then the possibilities for a solution are opened up rather than being closed down.

Discovery Exercise 1: Reality statement checklist

Objective: To use questioning to ensure your Reality statement covers all relevant areas.

Below you will find some questions to consider in defining your Reality statement. If one of the questions does not apply to you then skip it and go to the next one.

General questions
Is my Reality statement defined in the same terms as my Goal?

Is my Reality statement clearly related to how I have described my Goal?

Have I considered the steps I must take to achieve my Goal?

Which steps have I completed and which ones do I still have to complete?

How far am I currently from achieving my Goal?

Fact questions

Have I included relevant facts and figures about the current situation?

Is my Reality statement free of opinions and beliefs?

Is my Reality statement firmly based on my actual situation rather than on my fears and hopes about it?

Are there any assumptions in my Reality statement?

Have I included factual information about my previous attempts at this Goal and what happened?

Have I included details of anyone else relevant to my Reality?

Feeling questions

Have I included my feelings about my current situation?

Have I included my feelings about my Goal?

Am I being honest with myself?

How do I feel about previous Goal attempts which have not worked?

How do I treat myself when I hit setbacks?

Faculty questions

What skills and capabilities do I have available that will be useful to me in achieving my Goal?

What information or knowledge do I have that could be relevant?

Have I got any skills I can transfer from other areas of my life?

Have I ever succeeded at something like this before?

Not jumping ahead

Am I including information about Obstacles?

Am I focusing on where I am rather than what is stopping me?

Am I looking at where I am currently rather than where I would like to be?

(Please make a list of any potential Obstacles you discover, because we will need them in the next section!)

You have now completed the Reality section of the GROW process and the next stage is to look at the Obstacles that are stopping you achieving your Goal.

8

Obstacles

What is an Obstacle?
Why it is important to identify Obstacles
The different types of Obstacle
Obstacles and justifications
Listing your Obstacles
Obstacles audit

Reading tips
Be honest.
Think clearly.
Be brave.
Dig deep.
Be specific.

If you have been working through this book systematically you should already have defined your Goal and Reality statements. We now come to the point in the GROW process that you may have been longing for, or perhaps dreading: the Obstacles.

You may have found that when you produced your Goal and your Reality statement part of you was desperate to bring up the Obstacles. That part of you might have wanted to say something like: 'But I am too old/scared/don't have enough time/self-discipline, etc., to achieve my Goal.' Or you may have wished that the Obstacles would stay in the background and not have to be faced. In either case, this chapter is the place to get them out in the open and deal with them.

Before we go into detail about Obstacles, we want to repeat what we said in the Introduction about the importance of working through the GROW process in a systematic way. Having used GROW with hundreds of clients, we have learned that the process is most effective when you go through it stage by stage. This means not moving on to the next stage until you have fully completed the current one. This is often a test of will.

We recognise that this is not always easy. It runs counter to what we do in life. When we tell a friend about a problem we usually expect him or her to suggest solutions. So the idea that we should consider issues more deeply before we start looking at solutions is not what we are used to. But the power of the GROW process resides in how it systematically takes apart a problem before you get to the answers, so we ask you to be patient. Try to resist rushing on to complete the processes as soon as possible. Complete this Obstacles section as thoroughly as you can *before* you move on to Options and the Way Forward.

What is an Obstacle?

In GROW terms an 'Obstacle' is something that stands in the way of you fully achieving your Goal. In the process so far we have identified the end point, our final destination. This is the Goal with its defining moment. We have also acknowledged how far along the path we are to achieving our Goal – our Reality statement. In order for something to be an Obstacle it has to stop you, in some way, from moving from one point to the other.

119

Why it is important to identify Obstacles

Something hidden in the background

It is hard to deal effectively with an Obstacle when it is either not properly defined or lurking away in the background. When an Obstacle is in the open and you face it head on, you can apply a strategy to overcome it. The danger of not fully working through Obstacles at this point is that they return later to sabotage your efforts. The more you can identify them in this section, the better.

If your Goal is to be able to have a conversation in French with your boss and your current level is that you can speak only a few sentences, a block, or Obstacle, might be that you cannot afford to have French lessons. Or if you want to take up a new hobby an Obstacle could be that you are exhausted at the end of the day when you have free time.

It is good to identify Obstacles

The process of identifying Obstacles might appear to be a pessimistic one. You may think that because they are blocking your way they must be negative. In fact the very opposite is the case.

Unless you make a thorough job of identifying all your Obstacles now, they may emerge later at a stage when you least want them. That could be when you are putting all your attention into creatively considering your Options and progressing your Way Forward actions.

Once Bob was coaching a private client called Anne. She had just finished a long-term relationship and her Goal was to find a new partner. Despite using GROW intensively for two months, progress seemed slow or non-existent. In desperation Bob asked her, 'Is there *anything* else that might be blocking you?' Anne looked a bit bashful and confessed that she was still sleeping with her old boyfriend but 'just as friends'. This was the key to the problem, as keeping hold of the old relationship was preventing her letting go and finding a new partner. Once this was out in the open she could discuss it and decide what to do. In the end she stopped seeing her ex-partner and found a new relationship.

More Obstacles equals more Options

The other main reason for identifying as many Obstacles as possible is that in the next stage of the GROW process we are going to create Options for tackling them. So the more Obstacles you have, the more Options you get to create. Having a long list of Obstacles shows that you are really thinking through the achievement of your Goal and what is standing in your way. It demonstrates that your Goal is important to you and should certainly not be considered negative or defeatist. It also shows that you are prepared to dig deep and really treat this GROW process seriously. A short list could mean that you do not wish to face the truth, and this is often a reason why the same Goal might not be achieved time and time again.

The different types of Obstacle

Fears

Fears, of various kinds, emerged as the root cause of many Obstacles for the Test Team. Because our minds tend to shy away from anything that strikes us as fearful we avoid these difficult areas. This has the effect of making the fears worse. However, once fears become tangible facts they can be addressed effectively.

The fears of many Test Team participants were so wide and ill-defined that they could not think effectively about how to deal with them. As we worked to clarify these and help them, two types of fear emerged as the key causes of Obstacles.

Fear – of doing

The fear of doing happens when you sense that starting to deal with an issue will be difficult or painful in some way. One example was Megan's fear of sorting out her systems.

She was a high-flying management consultant and very successful at her profession. She joined the Test Team to sort out her administration and finance systems which were 'a gigantic mess'. She thought administration was so dull and boring that she could not possibly be bothered to sort it out. So the mess grew even bigger and had grown to the point where she was fearful to even look at it. This was costly to Megan as she had to use more and more of her time to find the things she needed to do her work.

Fear – of the results

Fear of the results comes about when we believe that achieving our Goal will adversely impact us in some way. Lindsey had run up large credit card debts in the past so her Goal was to get her financial situation under control. She earned a respectable salary but was constantly spending money on herself and her family without any real check on whether she wanted an item or could afford it. When she started to look at her Obstacles she realised she 'would rather bury her head in the sand' than face up to the Reality of her financial situation. In addition, she knew that becoming responsible for her money meant dealing with her judgements on herself for how she had behaved in the past.

Lisa's weight-loss Goal seemed fairly straightforward when she first presented it. Then, after the first week, she emailed us to say that a deep unexpected fear had surfaced. When she was in her twenties, she had been stalked by a customer in a shop where she worked. Then she was attacked by a friend she trusted. Her response to these events was to stay indoors and eat. She put on 70 pounds over two years as a defence against being seen as attractive.

As she put it, 'I know the slim me would like to get out of its protective padding but I am safer being overweight.' For her to lose weight would bring up all the uncomfortable and dangerous feelings she had avoided by putting on weight.

Our inner beliefs

We all have voices from the past that carry messages from our childhood or other life experience about the limits of what we can achieve.

Here are some examples from the Test Team:

I am not and never will be a linguist.

Susan

I am not practical or imaginative.

Donald

I am not competent in sales.

Marina

I am no good at finance.

Mia

By holding on to these beliefs we become trapped within fixed limits and never give ourselves space to find out what we can really accomplish.

There is a story of how baby elephants are tethered by a rope fixed to a stake in the ground. If the baby elephant tries to move further than the rope allows it will chafe its leg. So it stops trying to escape. When the elephant gets older it can still be tethered by the same strength rope and the same stake. Even though it is much larger now and could easily break the rope, it knows that if it tries to wander further than the length of the rope it will hurt.

We humans are very similar. We have our own ropes and stakes. We have learnt from the past that we can be hurt by certain situations or people so we tend to avoid them. The cost of this is that we never expand our possibilities and find out what life is like beyond the rope. Like the elephant, we are a prisoner of our past experience.

It is only by being aware of our self-imposed limitations and positively choosing to change them that we can move beyond what we have always accepted. It is not always an easy decision since the status quo has the advantage of being known. If we do choose to step forward into the unknown we then have the opportunity to discover our full potential.

Obstacles caused by other people

When other people are being obstructive it is easy to label them uncooperative, difficult or even ignorant. Once we have labelled someone in this way it is very tempting to look for the evidence that backs up our judgement, rather than the reasons behind their behaviour. This tends to make a situation worse, rather than improve it. Once we understand why someone is obstructing us we are in a position to start developing strategies that will get us a better outcome.

People obstruct us in a variety of ways. Sometimes they fail to co-operate in the way we would like. Or they may seem to be illogical, inefficient or fail to share our point of view. On occasion they might simply be unhelpful or not give us enough of their time.

Within the Test Team there were several instances where other people were a major Obstacle.

Paul, our IT specialist, had a boss who gave him contradictory instructions and asked him to act in a way which was against his own ethical beliefs about how you should do business. As Paul's Goal was to heal his stress-related heart condition this person was a significant Obstacle.

Matthew had to deal with people who insisted on speaking

English to him despite his repeated requests to have them speak Dutch.

Kayla needed to speak with commissioning editors who would not give her the time she needed to pitch her idea for a weekly column.

Other people can also be obstructive in less direct ways. Lauren noticed that whenever she spoke to her mother the conversation always returned to how she was ineffective at finding a partner and 'generally useless' in life. This was masked with a lot of concern about her welfare, but the end result was that at the end of the call she always felt demotivated and upset.

Obstacles caused by the environment

Environmental Obstacles include all the physical issues that interfere with you achieving your Goal. It could be the way your room is set up, how much space you have, any distractions of noise, visitors, telephones or email. All the physical things that get in your way should be included under this heading.

For example, when he was writing this book Bob noticed that his home environment was becoming an Obstacle. It was too easy to stop for a cup of tea, play with his son or check emails instead of continuing with the work. So he started to work for blocks of time in a library where he would not get distracted. This gave him the right physical space to work in and he was able to work more effectively.

Gabrielle wrote that there was always comfort food around where she worked which was difficult to refuse, and it was easier to drink coffee rather than have fresh water. So her environment was making it difficult to establish healthy eating patterns.

Obstacles caused by a lack of resources

In order to achieve your Goal you will need resources such as money, time, skills or knowledge. If you have the right resources you are in a much better position to realistically achieve your Goal.

If you do not have the resources you need it can seriously hamper you, as we can see from this example from Celia. Her Goal was to raise money for a hotel development. In order to do this she had to finish writing a business plan and send it to at least twenty interested parties. Although she was very enthusiastic about the project she lacked a number of resources. She had another job and did not have the time to devote to the project that it needed. Neither did she have committed financial backers. She was also aware that she did not know a great deal about property development. These limitations had a negative effect on how she related to the professionals who were involved, because she saw herself as an amateur, which made the situation worse. So Celia was lacking time, money and knowledge.

We have now examined in some detail the external and internal Obstacles that get in the way of us achieving our Goals. Before we give you the opportunity to look at your own Obstacles there is one key distinction we want to explore that will help you decide whether you are faced with a real Obstacle or not.

Obstacles and justifications

It may seem ridiculous to suggest that an Obstacle is not real. If a person has a fear it is certainly real to them. But Obstacles can be real or imagined, and the imaginary ones can feel just as hard and heavy as the genuine article. We noticed that some of the Obstacles the Test Team came up with were in fact justifications about why they could not achieve their Goal or why they could not even move forward. This led us to examine the difference between an Obstacle and a justification.

For the purposes of the GROW process we define an Obstacle as something that stops us moving towards our

Goal. A justification, on the other hand, is a belief you have about yourself or the world. Justifications come from our history and are an attempt to protect ourselves from repeating bad experiences.

For example, Nicole's Goal was to get her hand-made serving spoons into some key department stores. She thought one Obstacle was that 'My ex-husband will never let me be successful.' This was despite the fact that he was now 1,000 miles away and she had not seen him for a year. Because her husband had interfered a lot in her life in the past, she genuinely believed he would wreck her current ambitions.

We asked her how her husband could stop her marketing efforts when he was so far away. After a bit of a struggle Nicole acknowledged that he was not really stopping her. But even the thought that he might interfere again made her hesitant to move forward.

The GROW process is very useful when dealing with justifications because it highlights when an Obstacle is not real. By ourselves our minds go all over the place trying to find a Way Forward which will avoid pain and difficulty. By systematically addressing each Obstacle and asking if it is really stopping us, we are able to deal with them more effectively.

The Obstacle or justification test

Because we found justifications to be a real issue for the Test Team we devised a test which you can use to see if an Obstacle is real for you.

Discovery Exercise 1: Obstacle or justification

Objective: To uncover whether a statement is really an Obstacle.

The exercise is made up of just three questions that you can use to test whether you are confronting a *real* Obstacle

---

or a justification. Once you have something you suspect might be an Obstacle you can apply the tests to see if it is a real block or a justification.

Test 1: Is it a global statement?

What we mean by 'global' in the context of GROW is that we do not know what it refers to. Justifications tend to be global, or universal, blockers. Once you know what a statement refers to, you can question whether it is correct. Leaving it open means it cannot be questioned, which is our hidden purpose when making justifications! As we can see in the case of age, it sounds more plausible to say, 'I am too old' than to say, 'This is impossible.' In fact, both say the same thing.

You can test whether your justification is global by asking, 'What does that mean?' at the end of the statement.

Test 2: Is there a way round this?

There is no way round a justification. If we accept that it is true it becomes an insurmountable Obstacle which stops any progress towards a Goal dead in its tracks. If it was a *real* Obstacle, then the way round it would be obvious.

Let's take an example of needing to speak a foreign language to work in another country. We can test whether it is an Obstacle or a justification by asking: 'Is there a way around this?' If the answer is 'no' then your block is more likely to be a justification than an Obstacle.

As you *could* learn the language if only you put the time or effort into it, or as you could possibly use a translator, there is a way round the problem.

> **Test 3: Is it a real Obstacle?**
>
> Justifications do not represent clear Obstacles to achieving a Goal. This can be tested by asking, 'How does that stop me achieving my Goal?'

We can illustrate the tests with an example from the Test Team.

Jane's Goal was to find three alternative careers about which she felt passionate and inspired. She worked in finance and was fed up with the routine work she had to do and the uninspired people she had to work with.

Despite having this Goal, when we reached this stage the first Obstacle she listed was 'I am too old.' Let's apply the three tests.

Test 1: Is it a global statement?

We asked Jane, 'If you are too old, what does that mean?' Once she considered the question she was better able to identify the fears that lay behind the statement, that she would be rejected or not given a chance.

She was then better able to choose whether to let it stop her.

Test 2: Is there a way round this?

There is no way around Jane's age. It is a statement of fact.

Test 3: Is it a real Obstacle?

Jane's Goal was to identify three alternative careers, and it was not clear how being 'too old' stopped her from doing this. While it is possible that there may be jobs that have an age limit, until Jane has completed the first step of identifying the career she wants she will never find out whether her age is a true block.

So, having applied all three tests, Jane's example comes out as a justification rather than a real Obstacle.

Here is another example from two Test Team participants.

Caroline, as you know, wanted to get a major part in a film. Kayla was a journalist who wanted to be commissioned to write a regular column. When they reached the section on Obstacles they both identified the same apparent Obstacle – that their respective professions were 'very competitive'. Now it is true that both journalism and acting are indeed 'very competitive', but in strict GROW terms this is not an Obstacle.

Let us try our Obstacle or justification test on their statement 'It is a very competitive business.'

Test 1: Is it a global statement?

Question: And what does that mean?

Answer: Saying it is a 'competitive business' is just a statement of fact which can be applied to any field of business today. Of course, there are lots of ways to qualify this statement, but nonetheless it remains vague and unhelpful.

Test 2: Is there a way round this?

Question: Is there a way round this?

Answer: There is no way round this very general statement – it is at best a reminder of the market conditions, but in essence it is a fact that just has to be dealt with.

Test 3: Is it a real Obstacle?

Question: How does that stop you achieving your Goal?

Answer: For both Caroline and Kayla, although their business is competitive this should not stop them moving forward. In fact, this is more to do with a concern that they would fail than a real Obstacle which they could tackle.

On all three tests it was clear that the statement was really a justification. It might not be easy to achieve their Goal, but the fact that the business was competitive would not stop them.

Another simpler test is to imagine you were to be offered one million pounds for facing the fear you were avoiding. Regardless of the result, you would get a million for doing it. Would you still be holding back or would you be making that call? If a large enough reward is sufficient incentive for you to face the fear, the chances are that it is not a 'real' Obstacle which is really stopping you moving forward. You might need some creative Options to deal with fear and provide the necessary motivation, and we will show how to generate these in the next chapter.

Justifications are not completely irrelevant. They may well indicate a genuine fear. It is worth bearing in mind that they are there for a purpose – to keep us from experiencing pain, difficulty and frustration. But until we name them and address them for what they are they can have the effect of keeping us immobile.

Listing your Obstacles

Now consider your Goal and Reality statements and make a list of all the Obstacles you can think of that are standing in your way. At this stage don't make any judgements, just get them down on paper or on your computer without thinking too much. Remember the four key types of Obstacle:

- Obstacles within yourself – fears and concerns about taking action and the result of your actions;
- Obstacles caused by other people – the way they are and how they relate to you;
- Obstacles caused by your physical environment;
- Obstacles resulting from a lack of resources, lack of money, time, skills and abilities, information or knowledge.

The more open and honest you are with yourself, the more you will uncover the Obstacles that are particularly well hidden. Very often inner Obstacles are not clear to us initially. The first answer you get as to what is stopping you is probably only part of the complete picture. You have to dig a bit – and if you do, there is often a little 'Aha' moment when you discover the truth of a real Obstacle.

The next process will work best if you can be as specific as possible about what your Obstacles are. Sometimes when people first start looking at Obstacles they make a 'general' statement, such as 'Fear', which is so global that it is impossible to deal with.

Let's compare these two Obstacle statements: 'I am lazy' and 'I could get up earlier but I don't get out of bed until eleven each morning'. The former is a judgement and does not give us any useful information, while the latter tells us what is actually happening to cause the problem. The processes below will help you to clarify your Obstacles and turn them into useful information.

Involving your buddy or support group

The processes will help you to clarify your Obstacles and turn them into useful information. This part of the GROW process works well if you can do it with your buddy or support group. There is nothing to stop you completing it by yourself, but if you can get a chance to work with others we strongly recommend you do so. We have categorised each part of the process to make it clearer.

Discovery Exercise 2: Defining Obstacles with a buddy

Objective: To work with another person to uncover and validate your Obstacles.

First brief your buddy where you are in the process, or if you are both working on Goals agree this together.

Buddy asks	Buddy's response and action
'What is blocking you achieving your Goal?'	Give an answer; your buddy writes it down, saying, 'Thank you,' and nothing more. Try not to get into a discussion.
'What else is blocking you achieving your Goal?'	Buddy continues noting, thanking you for your answer and repeating the question again.

After you both agree you have established all the Obstacles then take each Obstacle in turn. Now the buddy asks a different question.

'How is .... [name the particular Obstacle] blocking you from . . . [the Goal]?'	Buddy notes your answer and says, 'Thank you.'

Example: If my Goal is to find a woman to come on a date with me, I may think one of my Obstacles is 'I am no good at conversation'. My buddy could ask, 'How is being no good at conversation blocking you finding a woman to ask out for a date?' So the exercise sheds light on why something is really an Obstacle and helps clarify the Goal.

Buddy repeats the question until both you and he understand how the Obstacle is stopping you from reaching your Goal. Then you move on to the next Obstacle.

If any of the Obstacles look remotely like justifications, remember to apply the Obstacle or justification test which we have outlined earlier in this chapter.

Take your time with this exercise, as the best answers seem to come after long silences.

It is also important to keep your Goal very much in mind; maybe it would be useful to have it written up on a large sheet of paper in front of you so you can both see it as the questions are asked.

If you cannot do this exercise with a buddy then you can do the process for yourself, but try to ask the questions in the same way. You could even record them and play them back to yourself.

Now, taking all your answers to the exercises in this chapter, write down your Obstacle statements.

ASK YOURSELF

Are these Obstacle statements about me, others, my environment or my Resources?

My Obstacle statements		
Obstacle	Type	Priority

Finally, see if you can prioritise your Obstacles in terms of what you currently think is the hardest to crack, the next hardest and so on. In this way you can see where you really have to focus when you come to identifying your Options.

Obstacles audit

Finally, here are some questions to consider about your Obstacle statement.

Discovery Exercise 3: Obstacles audit

Objective: To use questioning to uncover and test Obstacles.

Below, you will find some questions to consider in refining your Obstacle statements. If one of the questions does not apply to you then skip it and go on to the next one.

General

What is blocking me from achieving my Goal?

How do I know these things are really what is blocking me?

What else could be blocking me? (There are usually multiple Obstacles to difficult problems.)

What else could be blocking me? (Yes, ask again!)

Myself

How would I have to change personally to achieve my Goal?

What is preventing me changing?

How much do I trust myself to achieve my Goal?

What would I have to face that I do not want to, in order to achieve this Goal?

Am I doing anything directly or indirectly to contribute to/maintain the situation?

What risks or threats will I have to face in achieving this Goal?

Are the risks or threats real or a justification for inaction?

Do I have any expectations of how I should achieve this Goal?

Is that expectation blocking me? Am I considering the current situation or being influenced by past experiences?

Others
Are other people part of the Obstacles?
How specifically are they obstructing me?
What stops them giving the cooperation I want?
Am I assuming this or has it been verified in some way?
Are there groups or individuals involved who are making the situation worse?

Environment
If the Obstacles are in the environment (physical things):
Do I have the right physical environment to achieve my Goal?
What needs to change in the environment so that I can achieve my Goal?
What do I need that I have not got now?
What else might get in the way?

Resources
What resources do I need that I do not have now?
What skills and abilities do I need to achieve my Goal?
Do I have the time I need to achieve my Goal?
What financial resources will I need to achieve my Goal?
What knowledge or information do I need to achieve my Goal?

We suggest you do not do anything with the answers to these questions for the moment but use them in the next chapter.

So you have now been through the first three stages of the GROW process. You have chosen a Goal, know where you stand in terms of Reality and now hopefully have a good understanding of the Obstacles that are in your path and preventing you from going forward. In every question you are being challenged to consider and change. We really want to acknowledge all the effort you are putting in. If you maintain a level of commitment we are confident you will achieve your Goal. The hardest part is definitely behind you, and we are now going to move into the more positive territory of helping you create some Options and the Way Forward actions to your Goal.

9

How are you doing?

Reading tips
Check in.
Break patterns.

We wanted to take a pause in the GROW process at this point to check in with you. How are you feeling? You might be excited, cautious, optimistic, fearful, low, challenged. We recognise that the GROW process brings up a wide range of emotions in nearly everyone who uses it to achieve an important Goal.

All the participants in the Test Team experienced highs and lows as they worked through GROW. We noticed a significant dip in motivation occurred for many participants after they completed their Obstacles. There were two main reasons for this:

1 It can be discouraging to discover all your Obstacles and have no solutions (as yet).
2 GROW does not allow the 'escape routes' you use to evade difficult situations and you are forced to confront your habitual avoidance patterns. You then become demotivated to avoid having to face the discomfort.

If you are feeling that way at the moment we would like to help. We put this short chapter immediately after the Obstacles because we saw so many people become demotivated at this point. If you are feeling that you could use a boost, then we suggest you jump straight to Chapter 12 and read about how to recover your energy and enthusiasm. Then you can return to the next chapter and create your Options. If you are feeling fine then there is no problem and you can move on to your Options.

In Chapter 12 you will find:

- ways of discovering that you have lost motivation;
- an explanation of why you might have become demotivated;
- stories from the Test Team about their highs and lows and how they got through;
- a wealth of ideas and resources to guide you forward.

Low points are definitely part of the process, although we know when you are at a low point it is very discouraging. However, this does not mean that the Goal is impossible or that you should stop the process. The GROW process can be tough at times, but please remember: there is only one way you can fail and that is to give up. We know you can accomplish your Goal and achieve the success you deserve.

10

Options

What is an Option?
How you created Options in the past
Finding and using your different 'selves' to create Options
Other ways to create Options
Creating Options – the traps
Options audit
Choosing the right Options

Reading tips
Use creativity.
Make a choice.
Have fun.
Explore.

Having identified the Obstacles that stand in the way of achieving your Goal, you can now start to develop some Options for dealing with them. Without Options you would become stuck with your Obstacles and all the frustration that goes with them. Creating Options allows you to move forward.

The Goal section of the GROW process required a clear focus, and in the Reality and Obstacles sections you needed to be both truthful and factual. The Options section of the GROW process, on the other hand, is hugely creative and optimistic. It does, however, require you to answer a lot of questions. We know that when you come to your Way Forward you will find this effort worthwhile.

Some of our suggestions in this chapter might seem a bit off the wall. We ask you to trust us and the process and complete them as thoroughly as you can. These methods have been used by countless people to create strategies for overcoming Obstacles. They can work for you too. Remember what Einstein said: 'We cannot solve our problems by thinking on the same level that we have used to create them.'

What is an Option?

In GROW terms an Option is a way of dealing with an Obstacle in such a way that you can move forward towards your Goal. There is no right method for dealing with the Obstacles. Your Options could involve avoiding them, working through them or having someone else attend to them. The key point is that, once you have your Options, the Obstacle no longer holds you up.

How you created Options in the past

At this point it is useful to reflect on what Options you usually create when Obstacles present themselves. These strategies might well prove useful, but we also want you to consider different ones. When you know how you normally respond you are more likely to be able to make an alternative choice.

Approaching Obstacles

ASK YOURSELF

How do I usually *approach* Obstacles when they lie in my path? (Just note the first thing which comes into your mind and write it down.)

So how do you approach Obstacles? Warily, confidently, carefully? Do you get angry or frustrated? Or do you see them as a challenge?

Overcoming Obstacles

ASK YOURSELF

How do I usually *overcome* Obstacles? (Write down your thoughts about this then reflect on the type of words you have used.)

So, when faced with Obstacles, what is your strategy for overcoming them? Do you face up to them, tackle them head on or find ways round them, over them or even under them? Maybe you smash or dissolve them!

Your answers to these two questions probably reflect the way you approach and resolve problems or issues in your life generally. In this chapter we will offer many ways of creating Options so you have the widest choice in how you deal with your Obstacles.

Dare to be different

We are creatures of habit, and as such we usually find ourselves doing the same things in the same way. Routine is the name of the game; it is safe, secure and comfortable. It is also boring! In this Options section of the GROW process we will invite and encourage you to push out the boundaries and step off the well-trodden path. We will help you to create a better outcome than you would normally achieve, and possibly an outstanding one.

But to act outside the box you have to think outside the box. This is not the way most of us usually behave, so you will find us continually urging you to change your perspective and act from parts of yourself which might not always get the hearing and influence they deserve. We invite you to dare to be different, take a risk and change the patterns which may have held you back from making significant change for most, if not all, of your life. Such changes can involve some discomfort and fear, but the results are invariably refreshing and different too.

ASK YOURSELF

Am I prepared to experiment in this Options section, take a risk and dare to do it differently?

Finding and using your different 'selves' to create Options

Generally, in different life situations we act from a particular aspect of our character or personality, and they can be very different. It is like King Kong gently holding Fay Wray in the palm of his huge hand, revealing his 'gentle self', compared to when he shows his 'monster self' as he climbs the skyscraper waving away the menacing biplanes. We might show a different self to our children ('caring self') from the one we use at work ('efficient self'), although this can change in certain circumstances. We may use our 'efficient self' to prepare for a family outing and our 'caring self' for a colleague who has suffered a personal loss.

We have a large number of 'selves' at our disposal, but we generally use only a small number of them, with some being used rarely, if at all. We also tend to use the same 'self' in the same situation, so it is hardly surprising we get the same results. An alternative self might have an entirely different perspective from the one we choose out of habit.

Below, you will find a number of exercises and ideas to learn about your 'selves'. Once you have discovered some of the rich variety of 'selves' we all have available you will be able to use them in Discovery Exercise 2 to create a wide range of Options to deal with each of your Obstacles.

Use this Discovery Exercise as the first process in identifying some of your different 'selves'.

Discovery Exercise 1: My different 'selves'

Objective: To identify some of your various 'selves' which can be used to increase your Options and shift perspective as you progress through the GROW process

Make a list of your different 'selves'. These are what you act from in different circumstances and situations.

1 Ask others which of your 'selves' they see. Ask your partner, parents, workmates, your best friend, anyone who knows you well. But remember, this is a positive exercise, not a character assassination.

2 Evaluate each self in terms of how often you use it by writing in the third column either 'always', 'often', 'seldom' or 'hardly ever'.

'Self'	Circumstance or situation	Used (always, often, seldom, hardly ever)

Find the answers within

The second way of discovering 'selves' is to consider which parts you use when faced with an Obstacle.

ASK YOURSELF

Do I seek answers from my intuition when looking at an Obstacle?

Do I seek answers from my intellect when looking at an Obstacle?

Do I seek answers from my wisdom when looking at an Obstacle?

Do I seek answers from my heart when looking at an Obstacle?

Do I seek answers from my soul when looking at an Obstacle?

All these different parts of your identity can be used as 'selves' to help create Options in Discovery Exercise 2.

'Selves' from history or fiction

A fun way to create selves is to draw on personalities from fact or fiction. Pick a range of characters and put their names on sheets of paper. It might also be nice to draw them or paste an image of them on the sheet. When you come to Discovery Exercise 2 you can use them instead of one of your own 'selves'.

What Options would Bill Gates, Mother Teresa, Picasso and Henry VIII recommend? Or perhaps Mary Poppins, Superman, Darth Vader and the Three Musketeers? In picking your characters, consider what quality they bring. For example, is it their resourcefulness, courage, compassion or maybe their sense of fun?

You might be thinking, 'But I am not Bill Gates!' True! But we ask you to trust us that the perspective you get from pretending to be him (or anyone else) will still be valuable.

Use people you know

A last way of creating 'selves' is to decide what skills or abilities you need to deal with the Obstacle and to pick people you know in your life who have that skill. Put their names on sheets of paper. Of course, if you have set up your Support Group you can do this exercise with them.

Creating Options from Obstacles

You should now have a mass of 'selves' that you have discovered or invented. In this exercise you will use some of these 'selves' to comment, contribute and create some wonderful Options for your Obstacles.

Discovery Exercise 2: The Options circle

Objective: To create Options for Obstacles using your different 'selves'

1 Write one Obstacle you have identified in the previous chapter in large letters on a sheet of paper.

Options

2 Put this in the centre of a reasonable space on the floor. This is a physical exercise and you need to be able to move around. It can be done on a desk top but it is not nearly so effective.

3 Write the name of each one of the 'selves' on individual sheets of paper. So one sheet might be called 'creative self' and another 'determined self'. You should aim to have between five and eight 'selves'.

4 Set the sheets of paper out in a circle around the Obstacle sheet which you first put down. You may have developed far more than eight 'selves', and if this is the case try to consolidate them so you have no more than eight. Alternatively, if you find this difficult you can repeat the exercise with another set of 'selves'.

5 Stand back from the circle where you can view all your different selves and consider them carefully one by one. As you do so, try to take in a little of their different energies. Try not to focus on the situations where you usually use them. This will not be helpful as this is a totally different circumstance.

6 Choose a 'self' which feels inviting and step on to that 'self' with both feet. It does not matter if the 'self' you step on to does not seem immediately relevant – that is not the point. Each 'self' has something very particular to say about that Obstacle and their views and suggestions deserve to be heard. Remember that by employing these 'selves' you are getting out of your habitual ways of thinking, freeing up your creativity and unleashing new Options and ideas.

7 Look back at your Obstacle from where you are standing. Get a real sense of what it is like to inhabit that 'self'. Now, from that position, what Options do you have to offer in dealing with the Obstacle? It is important when acting from a particular 'self' to live it fully and not let your 'sensible self' interfere with the process.

It would be valuable to have your buddy or a member of your support group help you with this exercise. You can talk out loud and they can write your words down. If you are doing this on your own, we suggest you record yourself, play back the tape and write down your Options. If the idea of recording your voice as you go through this horrifies you, then that is precisely what you should do! Remember what we said about pushing out the boundaries.

Once you have recorded the Options created by the first 'self', move to another 'self' and repeat the exercise. You do not have to go through all your 'selves', so stop when you feel you have exhausted the process. However, it is important to visit as many different 'selves' as possible to create a wide range of Options for yourself. As you move through your 'selves' be aware of how you are feeling as you step on to each sheet of paper. Are there some places that you are happy to be in? Do you approach others with caution or with some discomfort?

ASK YOURSELF

How do I feel when I step into and work from a 'self' who seldom gets heard?

Here are some examples of a selection of Options from the Test Team when they did this exercise. You can see how easy it was to create action steps from the Options once they were discovered:

	Alan
Goal	To finish editing a film
Obstacle	I don't work well without pressure and there is no deadline

'Self' used	'Fun self'
Option	To create a fun way of putting pressure on myself
Action	Set a date for a viewing party and start inviting people now

	Sara
Goal	To decide whether to move in with my boyfriend
Obstacle	He does not give me enough freedom
'Self' used	'Fun self'
Option	To play with him
Action	Reward him with chocolate, which he loves, every time he allows me to do what I want

	Megan
Goal	To organise my administrative systems effectively
Obstacle	I do not know how to create good administrative systems
'Self' used	'Resourceful self'
Option	Find someone who knows about this to help
Action	Ask three friends, who are also consultants, how they created their systems

	Celia
Goal	To produce a business proposal for a new hotel
Obstacle	I do not relate well to the professionals involved because I think they do not take me seriously owing to the fact that I am not a professional in this field
'Self' used	'Direct self'
Option	Stop seeing it as a liability – use it positively
Action	Be honest, tell them that I am not a professional and ask for their help

There were numerous other examples of the insights gained by the Test Team from this exercise. As Linda put it: 'It is great to discover that there are so many more Options than Obstacles.'

Although the best Options can appear quite obvious, we do not always see them for ourselves. Others can spot them more easily. Bob has an example where he was trying to get a writing piece published and had been determined to get through to a particular magazine editor. He had phoned him thirty-four times without ever getting through. He told a friend, who suggested, 'Why don't you go round to his office?' Bob did and it worked. Now that might seem blindingly obvious, but at the time Bob did not see it because he had become so determined to do it his way.

Caroline gets creative

Caroline, the actor in the Test Team, loved using creativity and games. She used this exercise to create a lot of Options. We have included some of her posting to the web group about her

Options here because the way she created them was so inspiring. We think that you too will be inspired by them.

Hi everyone!

I really enjoyed the section about thinking of other people/ characters. As this is one of my main tools as an actress (I work from images a lot) I had a ball – and this is what I came up with.

I used the characters below to see how I could get over my inner fears and Obstacles about making contacts in the entertainment business.

Annica Bengtzon (journalist/heroine in Swedish crime novel)

Annica is persistent and never gives up till she gets to the bottom of a problem.

Annica is passionate about her job and temperamental – always breaking rules (sometimes inadvertently).

Annica has a good informant (this inspired me to get some good informants, too, who can give me information about the business).

Although all odds are against Annica at work, she has a senior manager who supports her and believes in her (inspires me to give an old teacher of mine a ring, he knows the TV business very well and I know he's very fond of me).

Annica is the person I want to be when making contact with people in the business.

Pippi Longstocking (the strongest girl in the world)

Pippi would walk into my agent's office when he's misbehaving, put him on top of the roof and let him sit there for a while.

Pippi makes me laugh, which reduces my agent's power (I feel empowered by this).

A computer hacker

A hacker would break into casting directors' computers to get all the information he needs (I will use the Internet to get as much information as possible).

Here are some of the Options I created to make the calls.

One Option is to try to break a few rules (to treat it as a playful game) and make myself feel more empowered. Casting directors don't like phone calls. But I can play on the fact that in Sweden they do. So I can say, 'Oh, sorry, but you see, where I come from . . .' In addition I have the Option of thinking that I can be as useful to them as they can be useful to me.

Another Option is to use these characters to make me feel less vulnerable. It will be a mask to wear, and not only a great inspiration but fun too! The Option here is to imagine what the characters would do in the situation and try out their methods. So far, inspired by this, I have sent out 160 letters, so I have 160 chances to get it right!

Option three: as English is my second language my Option is to see this as a strength rather than a weakness. To start selling myself as a Swedish actress (different, exotic, Ibsen expert) and reinvent my professional past in Sweden (expand on the truth, like everyone does anyway). This will give me the freedom to stick out from the crowd and be different.

Final Option: I realised I could make this fun instead of being so frightened. I'm going to draw a picture of a house with a garden on a big piece of paper, and when I call casting agents, for every positive reply I'll draw a flower in the garden, and for everyone being pleasant I'll draw a matchstick man sitting on top of the roof. (I'm Pippi Longstocking, the strongest girl in the world, after all!)

I will create that creative and fun space around me before I ring people up, because I believe they will pick up on my energy (the first five people I called were being ever so sweet)

– and that means that I probably have to allow myself to move forward a bit slower than planned. But one thing worked every single time: when I said: 'Do you mind if I ask you a question?' they all let me go ahead. I bet it threw them a bit . . . hee-hee.

Before we did this exercise Caroline had not thought of any of the ideas that she wrote about here. There is no rule that you have to be a 'creative' person to do the exercise well. That is simply another limiting belief. The exercise worked for Caroline and can certainly work for you.

Other ways to create Options

However you felt about this 'selves' approach from the first reading, we would strongly encourage you to give it a try. But if it really does not work for you, here are some other ways of creating Options from Obstacles.

Using questions

Take each Obstacle and ask some or all of the following questions. If you are working with your buddy, get him to ask the questions and write down your answers. Your buddy can also ask subsidiary questions if your answers are not clear, such as, 'What do you mean by that?' or 'How would that work for you?' Remember that your buddy is there to help you in this process, so try and be patient if his questions appear repetitive, difficult or intrusive. We want you to stay friends!

Discovery Exercise 3:
Creating Options through questioning

Objective: To use questions to create your Options

Instructions

Take each Obstacle and ask the following sets of questions to arrive at a workable Option.

Note which questions work best and try them first on your next Obstacle.

Process

What would be my first step?

What else could I do?

What would happen if I did nothing at all?

What is the simplest solution?

Abundance

If I had no limitations how would I handle this?

If I had a magic wand to use on this Obstacle, what would I do?

If I knew the answer, what would it be?

What is the perfect solution?

Shortage of resources

How can I create what I need?

Who could lend me what I need?

How else could I get it? Could I trade or offer something in exchange?

Who could I ask to get the information or knowledge I need?

How could I learn the skill that I need?

How could I create the time I need?

The tried and tested

Have I ever dealt with something like this in the past?

What did I do then?

What am I already doing now that works in terms of getting my Goal?

How can I do more of what is working for me already?

Is there a tried and tested way I can get around this Obstacle?
How could I find out about it?

Involving others
How would other people deal with this Obstacle?
Who do I know who could deal with this Obstacle well?
How would they go about it?
Are there any other groups or individuals who might be prepared to help me?
What mistakes have I seen others make?
How could I avoid making those mistakes myself?

About myself
What would really motivate me?
What would a change of attitude bring me?
Is there another part of myself that I can use?
What would I do if I were more assertive?
What would I do if I were less assertive?
What would be a real risk that I would be willing to take?
What would be a real risk that I would be unwilling to take?
How could I change my reaction to the situation or person to get a different result?
What rules am I operating under?
Am I sure they are true?
How could I deal with this Obstacle in a different way from my normal approach?

Quantity and quality
Do I have enough Options to move forward?
Do I have to solve this Obstacle at all or can I just avoid the negative consequences?
What would be a partial or temporary solution that would work for the moment?
What is missing?
What needs to be added?
What would a new approach bring?

If you get stuck on a particular question this could be a sign that it is irrelevant, but it might mean that there is something to be discovered. We would encourage you to stay at the point where you are stuck until you are sure the question has no value to you.

Take a 180-degree turn

There is nothing wrong with the conventional approach to creating Options if it works well for you. However, you might wish to explore a new process which will create some exciting and different Options. Here is a great opportunity to think and act outside the box.

Discovery Exercise 4: The 180-degree turn

Objective: To create radical Options

1 Write one of your Obstacles on a blank sheet of paper.
2 *ASK YOURSELF* 'How would I usually do this?'
3 Note the answer you come up with on your paper.
4 Now do a 180-degree turn and *ASK YOURSELF* 'What would the exact opposite of this be?'
5 Write down the first answer that comes up.
6 Repeat the question and write down more answers.
7 Sit with these answers and note your reaction.
8 *ASK YOURSELF* 'What can I learn about myself from these Options?'

Change your attitude

Sometimes it is possible to create an Option just by changing your mental attitude. For instance, Lindsey found she was always wanting to spend money when she went to social events in order to 'fit in'. She felt that the clothes she bought enabled her to 'wear a mask' and be safe. When she did our exercises Lindsey contacted her 'fun self'. This reminded her of how she used to be when she was colourful and lively and enjoyed standing out. She realised that standing out could be an Option for her once more. This, in turn, freed her from having to buy so many clothes, which helped get her spending under control – her original aim.

ASK YOURSELF

How could a change of attitude enable me to pursue a different Option?

Just believe it

Some of the Test Team felt that they did not have the confidence or could not quite believe it was possible for them to use some of the Options they had identified. Maybe you also feel this way. Don't worry, there is a simple solution. Just 'fake it 'till you make it'. By 'acting as if' you take on the belief of a confident person until it becomes a natural way of behaving.

ASK YOURSELF

If I were a confident person, what Options would I carry out?
Who do I know who is confident? What Options would they use to create action steps and how would they carry them out?

Creating Options – the traps

Here are some traps to watch out for when creating your Options and some ideas for avoiding them.

Are your Obstacles real?

It is worth referring back to your Obstacles and making sure that the ones you have identified are really stopping you getting to your Goal. It is very easy to take Obstacles from the past and project them into the future. For example, if you are trying to improve your appearance by buying some nice new clothes you might think an Obstacle is: 'My mother always told me that only stupid people spent money on expensive new clothes.' If you can, choose not to listen to the voice in your head that is not really an Obstacle. You might feel a bit guilty, but the voice is not actually stopping you buying the clothes, is it?

On the other hand, the belief that you don't know how to pick clothes that look good on you might be a genuine 'inner' Obstacle, which could be dealt with by creating some Options to get around the concern.

ASK YOURSELF

Does this Obstacle block me in some real way or stop me doing something that I need to do?

If it does, then it is a real Obstacle and you need to create an Option for getting round it.

Is your Obstacle specific?

Make sure you are creating Options for a *specific* Obstacle rather than a *global* one. Global Obstacles are statements such as 'I am not motivated' or 'I don't think I can achieve my

Goal'. Both these statements came from Test Team participants, and, as Obstacles, do not give sufficient information
for them to be properly addressed. Remember that clear
Obstacles usually give you some ideas for Options straight
away. If you are stuck, the chances are that your Obstacles are
not clear enough yet. Revisit the section on Obstacles versus
justification in Chapter 8 if you are not quite sure how to
clarify your Obstacles.

Options or Way Forward action steps?

If you are working on a Goal such as improving your relationships you might have an Option to improve your conversation
skills. Or you might find you create an Option such as 'I could
ask my best friend for some feedback on how I come across.'
The former is a Option that will take some development to
turn it into Way Forward steps. The latter is close to an action
step in itself and just needs you to put a date on it.

Not having enough Options

When considering any Obstacle it is tempting to take the
first Option that comes to mind, saying, 'OK, I have got one
Option, let's move on to the next Obstacle.' In doing so, you
are missing out on other possibilities. Although we do not
suggest you agonise over every one, it is important to stay
with the process long enough to really explore a number of
Options for each Obstacle. You then might find yourself
doing things in your Way Forward you had never imagined,
just because you were prepared to open up and consider
something new.

Choosing the right Options

Now hopefully you have created loads of great Options which are more than a match for those dreary Obstacles. You do not have to create an Option for every Obstacle. It is possible to move forward with some Obstacles still in your path. However, if some Obstacles are real blocks then these are the ones you simply have to focus on. You might have discovered some Options which do not relate to any of the Obstacles, and that is fine too.

Now comes the time to choose which Options you will use in your Way Forward section. Before you actually make your selection we would like to remind you of the importance of considering *all* Options and not just those you would naturally be attracted to.

Thinking and acting differently

At the start of this book we said that to make a major change in your life you need to think differently, otherwise you will always keep repeating the same patterns. At every stage of the GROW process we have been pushing at your boundaries and inviting you to change the way you normally respond. In going for your Goals you reflected deeply on what you really wanted in your life. In Reality you had to be totally open with yourself. The Obstacles work required you to question your perception of what stands in your way, and you have drawn on your creativity when considering Options.

We hope you have at least one Option which is a real challenge for you. You might not have a clue at this stage how you will move it forward. That is a sure sign that you have stepped outside what is ordinary for you. If this is the case, stay with the uncertainty and trust the process: you are sure to find some solutions here, and probably some great insights as well.

Criteria for choosing Options

The key to selecting an Option is to be sure that it will be useful to you in dealing with a particular Obstacle and moving you towards your Goal. Here are some ideas you can use to select which Option you carry forward.

ASK YOURSELF

Which of my Options would be:
  the easiest to implement?
  the most practical?
  most attractive to me?
  the most fun?
  most different from how I would normally behave?

The 'what the hell' method!

If you really do not know how to choose, you can leave it in the lap of the gods, providing you are prepared to live with the consequences. If you are really stuck, put all the Options in a hat and draw out the first three. Not scientific enough for you? Well, it certainly beats answering any more questions!

Discovery Exercise 5: Options audit

Objective: To review Options and decide which ones to choose. Look at your Options and ask the questions below.

Will this Option fit my timing?
Which Option would make the biggest difference to me?
Which Option is most like me?
Which Option is least like me?
Which Option would make me most confident I could achieve my Goal?
Which Option appeals to me the most, and why?

> Which Option would be most challenging for me?
> Which Option would produce the best result with the least effort/resources?

How many Options?

How many Options you take into your Way Forward is up to you. However, we would suggest that you aim to have about three *major* Options (you can have other minor ones). The reason for this is that if you have too many Options you lose momentum in trying to do them all. So select the Options that are going to make the most difference and take the others off the list.

My Options

Now you have created some clear Options that you can take on to the next chapter and your Way Forward. If you have answered even half of these questions, then we congratulate you.

Finally, before reading on, if you can bear it, here is just one more question.

ASK YOURSELF

What was my greatest insight when completing these exercises?

11

The Way Forward

What is a Way Forward action?
Creating Way Forward actions from Options
Selecting and refining Way Forward actions
Tracking and supporting progress
Way Forward audit

Reading tips
Make a commitment.
Be practical.
Take bold actions.

So finally we have arrived at the Way Forward, the action steps you are going to take to move confidently towards your Goal. In a sense this is the whole point of the GROW process, although by working through the other stages first you can be confident that the actions you take now will be successful. As we have said, the GROW process is like using a map when setting out on a journey. You have already defined your end point, the Goal; your starting point, the Reality; the Obstacles that are stopping you going straight from one to the other; and the Options for overcoming them. However, it is only by taking action that you are going to get your Goal, so the Way Forward is where you put into action all the great work you have put in so far.

In this Way Forward chapter we are again going to challenge you to act outside your usual patterns and boundaries. If you have a pattern of not giving yourself the best chance to succeed then this section is a great opportunity to change it. If you are usually pretty disorganised about the way you do things, create a clear structure; if you seldom work with others, involve them; if you do not usually create clear actions, we will show you how to do this effectively. If you are willing to accept this challenge you will be able to achieve your Goals in ways you never thought possible.

What is a Way Forward action step?

An effective action step will be clear, realistic and able to be completed within a short time scale. The key characteristics are as follows.

Attach a time scale

Every Way Forward action must have a date by which you are going to compete it. This also enables you to see if you have too many actions all with the same due date.

Keep it short term

The date for completion should be short term, by which we mean can be completed in one to three weeks. That way you get to see a result, which will encourage you with the other actions you are taking. If an action will take longer, see if you can find an intermediate step on the way and make that your Way Forward. Having achieved this you can then take another step, and then another.

Keep it clear

When stating your Way Forward actions it is important to be clear. The same rules we used to create a clear and measurable Goal also apply for your Way Forward, so it might be useful to go back and check them out in Chapter 6, 'Creating your Goal strategy'. It should be possible for anyone to understand what you have planned to do and confirm that you have done it.

ASK YOURSELF

If someone else read my Way Forward steps would they know what I meant?

Creating Way Forward actions from Options

It may be very obvious to you from reading your Options how you are going to create action steps. Indeed, some of your Options might already nearly be Way Forward action steps. This is fine, and maybe all you need to do is put a completion date on them. However, we would still encourage you to examine them in the light of the material in this chapter.

The simpler you make your Way Forward actions, the better. Here are two examples.

Suppose your Goal is to gain a promotion in your job. You have identified one of your Obstacles as not knowing the essential skills you need at that higher level. One Option would be to speak to people who are already doing the job and find out from them what skills they see as important. One Way Forward action step could be to list the people by name and make an appointment to talk with them.

Your Goal might be to speak another language and you have

a well-defined success point. Suppose you identified one Obstacle as not having enough conversation with native speakers. One Option might be to identify individuals who would be willing to help, and the Way Forward action steps would be to contact them and ask if they would spend some time speaking the language with you.

Processes for creating Way Forward actions

If you are having any difficulty creating action steps, here are two Discovery Exercises designed to help you create a long list of Way Forward actions. The first employs a process similar to the one you used with your different 'selves' to create Options. If you do not remember the exercise, we suggest you backtrack and revise it before trying this exercise.

Discovery Exercise 1: The action circle

Objective: To create Ways Forward using resource and action words

1 Make a list of action and resource words that might be useful to you in carrying out your Way Forward. You can use words like: contact, act, offer, information, support, knowledge, skill, clarify, request, remind, communicate, monitor, create, innovate and motivate. Then take some sheets of paper and write one of the words on each sheet. You can add your own words as well.

2 Put these words round in a big circle on the floor. You do not have to use all the words but make sure you include all that might be relevant to your Option.

3 Write an Option on a sheet of paper and put it in the middle of the circle.

4 Step on to one of the words in the circle and think about the meaning of that word in respect of the Option.

---

5 *ASK YOURSELF* How can this word help me create an action step?

6 For example, if you are standing on 'support', what support might you need as part of your Way Forward actions? If 'skill', what skill might you need to acquire? If 'communication', what do you have to tell others? If 'remind', who do you need to remind of what?

7 If there is nothing relevant for that particular word, step on to the next word in the circle and do the same.

8 Continue until you are sure you have enough action steps to ensure you can move forward with that Option.

9 Then take another Option and repeat.

With this technique you should get a good list of Way Forward actions. Remember that all action steps must be clear and able to be completed in one to three weeks.

Discovery Exercise 2: The power of nine

Objective: To create thorough lists of Way Forward actions for all Options

1 Take a blank piece of paper and draw two lines across and two lines down to make nine squares.

2 In the centre square write one of your Options. It is a good idea to give it a creative name: 'the juicy Option'. The more fun you have with this the easier it is to create actions.

3 In the remaining eight blank squares write eight different Way Forward actions for that Option, one in each square.

4 Review each of the eight Way Forward actions and number the squares 1 to 8 in terms of their usefulness in moving that particular Option forward.

5 If you have more ideas you can start another nine squares for that Option. One of the eight squares might well contain a Way Forward which is still too large to deal with straight away. If so, take another piece of paper, make nine squares and write that Way Forward in the centre, and find eight Ways Forward to progress it.

6 Repeat this exercise for all the Options – by now, if you are really going for it, you should be surrounded by pieces of paper. If you only have a few Ways Forward, challenge yourself to at least double these. Get your buddy or support group to help.

7 Gather all the action steps together, and later in the chapter we show you how to select the ones you will complete.

As you will see, Discovery Exercises 1 and 2 are actually different versions of the same thing. Exercise 1 ensures you consider all the different categories of Ways Forward available, and Exercise 2 looks at the Option and creates Ways Forward without any particular category being considered. You can combine these by doing your nine-box exercise with the Way Forward categories by your side as a prompt, to ensure that you cover all the categories.

As with the other steps, this part of the GROW process also works well if you can do it with your support group or buddy. There is nothing to stop you doing it by yourself, but if you do get a chance to work with your buddy get your own list of actions created *before* talking with him, and ask him to refine your actions and help you create more.

Selecting and refining Ways Forward

You should now have a wide variety of action steps you could take to put your Option into operation. We are going to show you now how to choose the most effective actions to lead you to your Goal.

How to choose your Ways Forward

Taking your list of actions from the Discovery Exercises you can ask the following questions. Which action steps would:

- be easiest for me to complete?
- produce the quickest result for me?
- have the biggest impact?
- not require any further resources or skills?
- be boldest?
- be outside my normal patterns of behaviour?

You can now select which action steps to take forward in the next couple of weeks. Be realistic about the amount of time and other resources you have available and how much extra effort each action step will take. To have the best chance of completing your actions it is important not to overload yourself.

ASK YOURSELF

Can I really carry out all these actions at the same time? Would it be better for me to stagger them?

Get committed!

Commitment is key. Sharing your intentions or decisions with third parties increases your commitment. They act as a witness and you are therefore less likely to fail if you risk letting others down as well as yourself. It should, however, be more than just telling somebody. It carries much more power if you say, 'I want you to witness that I . . .' Try it on something and see.

ASK YOURSELF

Am I fully committed to each Way Forward action I have recorded on my plan? Have I totally thought this through? Can I really see myself doing this?

In order to fully understand the Way Forward here are some examples which demonstrate how to create good action steps.

Transforming anxiety into well-defined actions

Marina wanted to recruit a sales manager for her agency but she had some concerns about her ability to recruit the 'right' person. We first clarified that 'right' meant someone who would fit into the team and deliver the required sales result. With this essential step completed, Marina's Options were to:

- create a more rigorous interviewing process better suited to this type of sales position, which was new to the company;
- have a large enough volume of candidates, in order to have a good number to choose from and avoid taking the first person available;
- find ways of reducing her commitment so that she could get out of any unsatisfactory situation relatively easily.

Marina's Way Forward

We decided to focus on finding a Way Forward for one Option, that of creating a more rigorous interviewing process. This could also be useful when hiring future staff for any position.

We used the nine-square process already described, with the words 'rigorous interviewing process' in the centre. The other squares Marina completed were:

- find someone who has recruited commission-based salespeople and ask their advice;
- find some sample interviewing forms for this kind of job;
- ask the advice of the Institute of Sales Management and other similar organisations;
- do some trial interviews with people who are from this area;
- make sure there is an appropriate application form;
- look on the web for more advice and information;
- make sure she describes her company working environment properly;
- identify how a salesperson would fit into that environment and consider them working from home.

In working through this process Marina had an important insight. She had set up her business on her own many years ago and did not routinely think of asking for help from others or look for information outside her own experience. This was an approach which could probably benefit other areas of her business. In addition, once she had clarified her anxiety about recruiting the 'right' or 'wrong' salesperson the fears were virtually eliminated.

In Marina's case we moved her unclear subjective fears into clear objective plans. Also, by working thoroughly through the GROW process Marina had created far better Ways Forward than she would otherwise have done.

Getting practical

Looking at her Obstacles, Caroline, our actor, realised that her current agent was not giving her the best chance of work, so a key Option for her was to find another one. Here are her twelve Way Forward actions for achieving this. As you read them, notice the verbs, 'sending', 'researching', 'reviewing', and so on. Also notice how much she is involving others to give her feedback, support, contacts and advice. You will also notice that everything has a date.

Caroline's Way Forward

1 Make creative space and ring up ten casting directors every weekday morning. (That's 110 casting directors by Friday 26 March, with three mornings off.)

2 Meet up with or ring a friend for support every day up to Friday 26 March.

3 Arrange a meeting (in person or over the phone) with director X to get professional support by Sunday 14 March. (He is a senior director, a wonderfully generous and wise man. I've worked with him in the past – he will hopefully be my 'informant'/give me some clues about how to get into the business.)

4 Ask at least three other actors about their relationship with their agent and get some tips about contacts by Friday 19 March.

5 Attend one casting class at The Actors' Centre by Friday 26 March. Not only is the class itself valuable, because you get a chance to rehearse the casting process, but the teacher also runs casting sessions for an agency and I would like to ask him for advice about how to get in.

6 Speak to my agent twice a week (at least . . .) up to Friday 26 March.

7 Make sure I reward myself properly once a day up to Friday 26 March.

8 Ring *Spotlight* to get names of agents that might be suitable by Friday 2 April.

9 Ring X and Y (casting directors at the BBC) to ask if they are still happy to act as my reference by Friday

---

2 April (they kindly offered this at a casting about a year ago).

10 Get footage from classes at The Actors' Centre that might be suitable for a new show reel by Friday 2 April.

11 Find out if directors I've worked with in the past are represented by agents, and if so use them as a way in if possible by Thursday 8 April.

12 Review my show reel and more recent footage with my actress friend Katrine to get ideas for new show reel by Thursday 8 April.

Tracking and supporting progress

While it is extremely important to select the action steps which will make the most difference it is also important that you keep track of your progress and create good support structures. Here are a few ideas.

Visual checks

These could include:

- tick lists on the wall;
- maps with action steps on them;
- computer-generated reminders;
- asking your buddy to call you.

ASK YOURSELF

How do I usually keep track of things I have decided to do? Does this work for me or do I need to find another method?

Using support

If you have a support group or buddy process in place you can check out your Way Forward actions with them. In any case it will be important for them to have a record of your planned actions for a number of reasons. If they know what you have planned to do they can actively monitor where you are on your actions at agreed times. This does assume you are happy with someone doing this and will respond well, even if you have not done what you intended.

Way Forward audit

Now you have selected your actions use this checklist to review them. The ideal is to have a combination of Ways Forward which will virtually guarantee success. The questions will stimulate your thoughts and increase the range and scope of your actions.

If you have already taken some action and it is not working, you can use these questions to get back on track again.

Discovery Exercise 3:
Questions to identify Way Forward actions

Objective: To test and expand Way Forward actions

Actions
What is the first action step I need to take?
How can I work forward from my first action to the next step I must take?
Do I need to:
    make a contact?
    acquire a new skill?
    gain knowledge?

---

take an action to change a pattern?
take an action to remind myself of my Goal and process?
do something physical?
complete something?
monitor something?
ask for something?
offer something?
What is the last action step I must take?
How can I work backwards from the last action to the first step I must take?

Completeness
Are my Way Forward action steps realistic?
Have I considered all the Options that might be useful?
Is this Way Forward action something I would have done in the same way without the GROW process or reading this book?
Could I do more than I am going to do?
Am I trying to do too much?
What would be a bold or adventurous action for me?
What would be a creative action?
How could I take action on my biggest challenge?
Have I built in ways to stay motivated?
Are there any vague adjectives like 'wrong', 'right', 'good', 'bad' in my Obstacles and Options?

Support
What support do I need?
Who might be willing to help me?
How and when am I going to get that support?
Can my buddy support me?
Where is the first place I would think of looking for support?
Where is the last place I would think of looking for support?

Consequences
Who will be most affected by my Way Forward action steps?

Do I need to inform them?

How will I cope with any adverse reactions from other people?

Commitment
On a scale of 1–10, with 10 being totally confident, how confident am I that I will carry out all my Way Forward actions?

If less than 10: do I need to adjust the tasks or time scale to have more certainty?

Do I have any considerations about my ability to carry out the action steps?

If 'yes', how can I get around them?

Completion
By what date do I want to have achieved each Way Forward action step?

Are my Way Forward action steps in a SMART format? (Specific, Measurable, Achievable, Relevant, Time Phased)

Am I satisfied that the Way Forward action steps will enable me to achieve my overall Goal?

How am I going to celebrate my achievement?

Well done. You have completed the last stage of the GROW process and all that is left to do now is to carry out your actions and achieve your Goal. If only it was as simple as that! But we all know we have to maintain motivation and self-discipline or we will never get that Goal. It also helps if we can inject some fun and joy into the process to lighten the load. So in the following chapters we offer you some help to complete the final stretch.

12

Staying motivated

If you are stuck
What is motivation?
How to know when you have lost motivation
Why you become unmotivated
How to recover your motivation and maintain progress

Reading tips
Be patient.
Be determined.
Be willing to ask for help.
Stay open to the practical suggestions.
Watch out for 'Yes, but . . .' and 'This will not work for me.'

If you are stuck

Welcome to this chapter on staying motivated. You may have worked through this book in the order in which it was written or jumped forward to this point. Either way is fine. This chapter is designed to help you whenever you need it.

Help! There is no way out

In conducting the Test Team programme we discovered that, while many Goals seemed straightforward at the outset, there were often hidden issues which led to participants feeling unmotivated. So we wrote this chapter because we saw people going through difficult periods while working through GROW. There is a very good reason for this difficulty. GROW is so effective because it leaves no room for our habitual avoidance behaviours. Generally, when we are faced with a task that appears hard or potentially painful, we can make excuses, procrastinate or distract ourselves to avoid the perceived difficulty. These are typical 'escape manoeuvres'. Because GROW is so logical and direct we cannot sustain the normal justifications that stop us taking action. 'GROW gives me no room for my usual excuses and evasions,' said Susan. Normally we are very good at justifying our inaction. When we start to use GROW our minds begin to feel threatened because we can no longer rely on our usual 'way out'. So, in an effort to stop the uncomfortable feelings, we start to feel unmotivated.

'This will not work for me!'

If you feel you are having difficulties, then this is not a sign that this book will not work for you. It is more likely to be an indication that the GROW process is affecting you on a deeper level than you are used to. When you are unmotivated it is tempting to 'throw in the towel' and give up, but that simply keeps the status quo in place.

It would be fair to say that everyone, including Chris and Bob, suffered periods when they lacked motivation during the programme. Take heart! Low points are not necessarily a bad sign and there are ways through them.

We were proud of the fact that, out of a fairly random sample, only six of the original forty-three participants in our Test Team did not complete the programme. Interestingly, five of those six left after the introductory session. The remaining thirty-seven people were excited by the process and the results they achieved. They stayed to the end, despite experiencing moments of depression, low energy, doubt, self-criticism and uncertainty. If at times you feel resistant to the process or find you can't do your action steps then you are not alone. Here are some comments from the Test Team about their low moments:

> I thought I was the only one to have been feeling STUCK STUCK STUCK this last two weeks but it seems that I am not.
>
> Susan

> I worked on my Options and the more I did this the more desperate I felt.
>
> Erika

> After proudly announcing that I could face all my Obstacles on the Monday teleclass I had a breakdown on Wednesday and sat paralysed at home for the whole day.
>
> Nicole

> The Obstacles part of the process brought out loads of old beliefs and I felt like I was drowning in fears.
>
> Caroline

In the first half of this chapter we describe how to know you are demotivated and why it happens. In the second half we describe how to deal with lack of motivation. Our Test Team have also given some encouragement and advice from their own experiences, which you can read in Chapter 1, 'The GROW Test Team'. We hope you will find their input useful and supportive.

What is motivation?

If we are clear on what we want and there is no problem about how to achieve it, then we do not usually have to worry about motivation. For example, most of us have no motivation problems regarding eating – there is food in the fridge and we don't have to feel motivated to get it out and eat it. No, motivation is only an issue when an activity seems an effort. You might say: 'I have lost my motivation to go to the gym.' In other words: 'Going to the gym requires an effort and I do not have enough motivation to get past that.' Alternatively, if we play in a sports team we could be very motivated to win even if it requires a lot of effort. How motivated we are depends very much on the circumstances. In this chapter we show you how to create the most favourable circumstances to stay motivated.

How to know when you have lost motivation

There are a number of ways to recognise that you are unmotivated. Here are some of the 'symptoms' noticed by the Test Team:

- lacking excitement and anticipation about the Goal;
- finding it hard to work through the GROW process;
- finding it hard to carry out Way Forward actions;
- being self-critical;
- lacking energy;
- finding it hard to concentrate.

Another indication of low motivation is using the phrase 'I should' about actions you have not completed. The phrase 'I should' is very important. What it means is that part of you *does* want to do something and part of you *does not*. But you do not usually see it that way. It feels as if you are caught between these opposing forces and unable to move. While you may think that the part of you that says 'I should' is in control, it is actually the part that is *resisting* that is in command. You can tell this because the resistant part usually wins (at least in the short term)!

Once we tell ourselves we 'should' do something it becomes much harder to complete it because we are ignoring the part of us that does not want to do it. This is important to understand, because we make life a lot more difficult if we start fighting ourselves rather than allowing all parts of ourselves to work together.

ASK YOURSELF

Am I using 'I should' when thinking about achieving my Goal?

Why you become unmotivated

In our work with the Test Team and from our own experience we have discovered many reasons that cause us to feel temporarily demotivated. Maybe you can identify with some of these too.

We don't realise that we are lacking resources we need

We can lose motivation because we are missing some skill, knowledge or resource we need to reach our Goal. This causes us difficulty as we are not fully aware that we need it.

Marina was finding it hard to recruit a new manager for her business. It seemed there should be no problem in identifying the right person but she was not making much progress. In a teleclass we probed to discover the reasons and she had a moment of realisation.

'But of course no one has ever taught me how to interview someone,' she exclaimed. Up to that point she believed she should use her instinct to magically divine who the best person was.

ASK YOURSELF

Am I missing any key information or knowledge that I need to complete my Goal?

There is a hidden agenda – I want to do it, but . . .

Tiffany's Goal was to clear up her flat and establish some systems to look after her money. This seemed like a straight-forward objective, but halfway through the programme she found herself totally stuck. Her ex-partner used to keep the place tidy and deal with the paperwork, but now he was gone and she felt an enormous resistance to continuing the work herself. Here is how she described the situation after one unproductive weekend when she could have cleaned up the apartment.

'I had time to do it and did not do it. I should do it, I haven't done it, I am a stupid person. I don't really want to take responsibility for these issues. I don't know how to make myself do it,' she said.

On the face of it the Goal was straightforward, but there was a second part that she was not completely aware of. The Goal would more truthfully have been written as 'I want to have my flat cleaned up and my paperwork sorted out *but I don't want to do it myself*'.

It is the second part of the Goal (after the 'but') which has greater importance because, on an unconscious level, we are more committed to that than the first part (our Goal). The unspoken or unwritten part has more power over us than our desire to achieve our Goal.

If you are having difficulty with your Goal it may be that you too have a hidden agenda, just as there was for Tiffany. You can tease these 'second parts' out by adding 'but . . .' to the end of your Goal and then completing the sentence. Here are some more examples:

I want to get a lead part in a film *but* I don't want to have to sell myself.

I want to earn £100,000 *but* I don't want to have to work eighteen hours a day.

I want a promotion *but* I don't believe my boss will ever recommend me.

By making the second part of your Goal explicit in this way you will discover any hidden agendas. Once you have uncovered them you can treat them just like an Obstacle, but while they remain hidden they have the power to disrupt you.

Another hidden agenda – what are you afraid of?

The second way a hidden agenda can interfere with your GROW process is similar to the first but looks at one specific aspect – hidden fears, which are not being expressed. While we might be conscious of some of the fears we may have to encounter while achieving our Goal, there are often deeper hidden ones affecting us.

This type of deep but unformed fear can hold us up. The test for this type of Obstacle is to put 'but I'm afraid that . . .' after the Goal. So, 'I want to learn to be more creative' becomes 'I want to learn to be more creative *but I'm afraid that* I'll find out I am no good at it.' The hidden fear is drawn out in the second part of the sentence.

A final hidden agenda – in order to . . .

The third way that a 'hidden' second part of a Goal can lead to demotivation is when we anticipate a consequence for the Goal that may not be true. This can be tested by using the phrase 'in order to'. For example: 'I want to have a new house *in order to* make my wife and children happy.' If your Goal is to make your wife and children happy that Goal may not actually be achieved by buying a new house. If you are working towards that Goal you will become unmotivated if your family does not respond to your efforts in the way you would like.

Finding those hidden agendas for yourself

So revealing the hidden second half of the Goal is extremely useful because it:

- points very clearly towards where the real issue is;
- brings out any hidden fears you might have;
- shows you where you might be going down a 'false' route.

Discovery Exercise 1: Finding hidden agendas

Objective: To uncover hidden agendas, fears and false routes

1 Write down your Goal at the top of a blank sheet of paper.
2 Put 'but' on the end of it and complete the sentence with as many 'buts' as you can.
3 Take a second sheet of paper and repeat the exercise using 'but I'm afraid that'.
4 Take a third sheet of paper and repeat using 'in order to'.

You will then have three lists of hidden Obstacles, fears and agendas.

ASK YOURSELF

For the 'but' statements: Is this a real Obstacle for me? If it is a real block then you can treat it as such.

For the 'but I'm afraid' statements: How real is this fear to me?
If it is significantly holding you up then re-read the section on fears in Chapter 8, 'Obstacles'. Also, in Chapter 10 you will find a Discovery Exercise about 'Creating Options through questioning'. Here you will find many useful tips to help you deal with fear. If you decide the fear is not real, then ignore it.

For the 'in order to' statements: Am I sure that achieving this Goal will give me what I want? If the answer is 'no' you may wish to revisit the chapter on creating your Goal statement and set a new or modified objective.

How to recover your motivation and maintain progress

Imagine for a moment that you are a shareholder in a company that has been making steady profits. If the profits started to slow down or turn into losses you would expect the management team to take action. You would want them to find out what has happened and implement changes to get the company profitable again and protect your investment.

Let us now imagine that you are the company. You are also the management, and the slow-down in growth described above is you becoming unmotivated. Ideally, you would tackle this in the same way that a company would. First you would find out what has changed and for what reason, and then you would take corrective action and regain your forward momentum. Unfortunately, we are generally not good at managing ourselves. We tend to get caught up in destructive cycles of blame and recrimination rather than taking a measured and logical approach.

So how can we learn to be better 'self-managers'? Below, you will find lots of quick self-management tools that you can pick up and use any time you find yourself not moving forward as fast as you would like.

Use your own resistance

When we get stuck, one of the most powerful ways we can change the situation is to have a dialogue between our different parts. This is not always easy to do as our minds can convince us that there is no point in even trying. Our minds and negative self-talk can be very convincing. But we do not have to believe what we hear – unless we want to.

Use your own 'stuck situations' as an opportunity to deal with this pattern once and for all. It may not be easy. You will have to change the way you handle being stuck. Instead of running away from uncomfortable feelings you will have to start deciding, instead, that you want to address them.

The following exercise builds on the 'selves' process we explained in Chapter 8, so if you have not completed that yet, you should read or revise it before attempting this exercise.

Discovery Exercise 2: Finding your 'stuck' part

Objective: To visualise the 'stuck' part of ourselves

1 Imagine in your mind's eye the part of you that is 'blocked' and does not want to continue. It is useful to picture it as having a physical shape and a personality. Here are some questions which will help:

Does it have a physical shape? If so, what is the shape?
What colour is it?
Does it have a body? If so, what does it look like and what position is it in?
What age does it seem to be?
What emotion is it expressing?
2 Find a word or phrase that sums up how it feels. Perhaps something like 'I'm fed up', 'I can't' or 'Leave me alone.'
3 Take a sheet of paper and draw a picture of that part and/or write the word or phrase on the paper.

When Bob did this exercise his 'stuck' part was a small boy sitting with his arms crossed, scowling and saying, 'I will not!' in a petulant voice.

Here is the second part of the exercise.

Discovery Exercise 3: Communicating to your 'stuck' part

Objective: To learn how to communicate between different parts of yourself

1 Choose some 'selves', as we described in Chapter 8, which might be helpful to you, and set them out in a circle surrounding the 'blocked' self in the centre.
2 Choose one of the outer selves and stand on that piece of paper. Face the centre of the circle and ask the 'blocked' self one of the following questions:
What do you need?
What would allow you to start again?
What is painful or difficult for you?
How can I help?

3 Move to the centre of the circle and stand on that piece of paper while you let the 'blocked' part reply.

4 Have a conversation with your 'blocked' self in an attempt to free up the 'stuck' situation. If you find that one of the outer 'selves' is not working or you have gone as far as you can, move round to the next.

5 Use as many of the outer 'selves' as you need for this exercise. Stop as soon as the 'blocked' self feels heard and is ready to allow progress again.

Here is part of a dialogue which Bob had with himself:

Creative self: How can I help you? It looks quite painful being stuck.

Blocked self: I don't want to write this chapter – it feels too difficult. There is no one to help me. I want to stop. [fed-up whiny voice]

Creative self: Have you thought about making it more fun – what about asking someone round to help?

Blocked self: All my friends are away and anyway I want to solve this myself.

Creative self: What about a treat when you are finished?

Blocked self: I don't want treats later – I am fed up now!

Bob moves to 'Determined self'.

Determined self: How can I help?

Blocked self: I need some help to get on with this – it just seems overwhelming. [sounding a bit sad]

Determined self: If you must do this alone, how about working for half an hour solidly and then stopping?

Blocked self: That seems too long – I can't manage more than 15 minutes.

Determined self: OK, let's settle for 15 minutes solid and then have a break, but let's make it 15 minutes of real work. Then you can go for a short walk or do something else you enjoy.

Blocked self: OK, 15 minutes. [sounding relieved]

The result of this short exchange was that Bob was able to work for two hours and finish off the chapter. Once the 'blocked' part felt heard and some negotiation had taken place, the log jam was broken.

You might find it helpful to do this exercise with your buddy or a friend who can give ideas and support. The concept of having a conversation with yourself may seem strange but, as we said before, we have many other 'selves' available to us, we just don't use them. When we do decide to use them we access a great source of inner wisdom and information.

Finding the fun way

When we feel trapped in doing parts of our Goal that we do not enjoy, one creative way to deal with them is to make them fun. When Chris had to do sales 'cold calls' he used to create a game whereby every time he had worked for 30 minutes he would stop and give himself a small treat, like a sweet. To remind himself he would put the sweet by the clock, so that when it was the right time he could eat it straight away.

Kick-start yourself

It is a common misconception that when we are unmotivated we have to find an incentive that will motivate us right up to the point when we finish the job. In fact, if we find a motivation that will work for, say, the next half hour, very often we are then able to keep going. As we saw when Bob had difficulty writing this chapter, he elected to do a 15-minute burst, but once he got started he stayed writing for two hours.

ASK YOURSELF

What would motivate me for the next 10 minutes?

Susan told us in a teleclass how much she enjoyed making learning fun for her children, but she had never thought how to do the same for herself. Once she realised this, she started to bring her creativity to the GROW process. She made her 'to-do' lists more visually interesting, used games to create some fun while carrying out her actions and planned her route to success on a 'map' on the wall, with pictures and rewards.

Delegate the detail

Some people enjoy producing complete reports with accurate cross-references and a perfectly consistent layout. For them, attending to detail is a pleasure. But perhaps you are the type who enjoys creating ideas and concepts but finds it difficult to get down to the detail required to put ideas into action. If you are, then it is likely you will feel unmotivated at having to do detailed work.

Perhaps what you need to do is find someone who is good at it. While this might have a cost, you could also look at creative arrangements like skill swaps instead of paying with money.

This is also a good opportunity to make an exchange with your buddy. Somehow it is easier to do other people's detail!

Acknowledge the progress you have made

When we find ourselves stuck it is very common to feel that we have not achieved anything at all. At these times it is a good idea to write down what you have actually done. Why not try this now? The blanket assertion that you have not got anywhere is rarely true. When the Test Team wrote down the progress they had made, many were surprised at how much they had accomplished.

Be open about your situation

When we are stuck it is tempting to keep our situation a deep dark secret. Lauren wrote: 'As I was writing down my Obstacles I thought that I should not be as open as this. But being open has actually made me more liberated and made me more motivated to get my Goal.'

Build momentum

If you find yourself faced by a large, seemingly insurmountable task, then break it down into the smallest chunks you can. Then start doing some of these really small bits. If you break things down to the level of making a phone call or setting up a file, most of us can manage to do some of these actions. Once we have started we can then look at how to keep the momentum going.

ASK YOURSELF

Could I break down that difficult task into smaller steps?

Often doing a large task is like moving a supertanker – starting is the hard bit. Once it is going it is easier to keep it going.

Get support

We saw from the Test Team that those participants who were best at asking for support were also more likely to achieve their Goals. When we are unmotivated, support is particularly valuable because:

- other people do not have our history so they can think more clearly about the issues than we can – they can be objective;
- they can distinguish 'fact from fiction' for us;
- they do not share the same feelings of guilt and blame we might feel when we have not done something.

Developing support networks is a key skill for staying motivated. If you revisit Chapter 4, 'Preparing the ground', you will find a detailed plan to set up a buddy system or support group.

ASK YOURSELF

Do I find it easy to ask for help?

If you do not find it easy and you have not done so, now is a good time to find some support.

Reaffirm what the Goal will do for you

Sometimes people get demotivated because they lose touch with why they wanted their Goal in the first place. One way of reconnecting with this feeling is to imagine reaching the 'defining moment' of your Goal.

> ### *ASK YOURSELF*
>
> How will I feel when I have achieved my Goal?

See if the feelings are still as vivid as when you set out. If not, you might want to reassess your Goal and replace it with something that is more compelling for you.

Unsticking questions

Here are some good questions to move you forward.

> ### *ASK YOURSELF*
>
> What do I want right now?
> What would be a first step I could do?
> What would enable me to move forward?
> What am I avoiding?

Keep asking these questions until you feel you have arrived at some resolution.

Keep a record of the times you are unmotivated and the times you are not

You might think while you are feeling unmotivated that the stuck situation has gone on for ever. The chances are that there have been times when you felt more motivated than you do now. There may also have been times when you felt even less motivated, but you came through them. If you map out the times when you were motivated or unmotivated you may see some patterns start to emerge. Look closely at these patterns and see if they help you to work out what is causing your current lack of motivation. This is a good opportunity to use the journal that we suggested you keep. If you have not got one, now is the right time to start. You can find the details in Chapter 4, 'Preparing the ground'.

Forgive yourself and move on

This is probably one of the most powerful tips we can give you on the subject of lack of motivation. Lisa said, 'If you slip up, acknowledge it.' Say something like, 'I slipped up today but I can start again tomorrow.' This is better than saying, 'I slipped up and am going to walk away from it.' This kind of positive self-talk frees you from guilt and allows you to move on. (There is *no limit* to the number of times you can do this!)

ASK YOURSELF

What do I have to forgive myself for right now?

If the immediate answer is 'nothing' stay with the question a little longer and see what comes up.

Allow yourself to 'wallow'

Iris had a sure-fire way of dealing with demotivation.

'When I feel myself going into "poor me" or feeling a lot of self-pity I consciously choose to indulge myself for half an hour,' she said. 'I lie on the bed and cry or hit a pillow and write down how miserable I feel. This allows me to experience those feelings for what they are for a while and then move on.' Paradoxically, consciously choosing to really have these negative feelings can release us from them.

Learn to be kinder to yourself

Often the pressure we put on ourselves when we do get stuck makes the situation dramatically worse. Here is a dialogue from a teleclass which illustrates the point beautifully:

Sara: Always having to be perfect really blocks us from seeing things the way they are and treating ourselves nicely and with kindness.

Bob: We don't need perfection.

Nicole: That might be a bit of my problem too.

Michelle: But if you don't give of your best you could fail!

Bob: What would it mean if you failed – that you are not good enough? What would you say to a child if they were experiencing this issue?

Michelle: I would say to my son, 'Try again or try something different'.

Bob: What do you think he learns through failing and being encouraged to try again?

Michelle: That you survive. That you learn from your mistakes. That you learn that it is OK to fail.

Bob: Yeah, really good. Why do we not say that to ourselves?

Lindsey: Time frames put on the pressure.

Bob: What would a child say in that situation?

Lindsey: It's fine, don't worry about it. But I think I will get into trouble if I don't deliver and let people down.

Bob: It is about being OK if something does not work. We think if something does not work that we are a failure and a bad person. We can carry on punishing ourselves like that for ever, but it is very costly. Not only do we not get what we want but we get to feel really bad about it, and about ourselves, too. What about some celebration of our learning?

Tiffany: Some of the things we have been talking about are real triggers for me. Particularly the comments about perfection. I am getting a bit lost. I have a lot of pressures at work. It is never good enough. I always think it could be better and I never feel I have really done my best. I can't really enjoy anything I have achieved as I always think it could have been better.

Bob: If you were talking to a child and suggesting that whatever he may have done he could have done better, how do you think that child would feel?

Tiffany: Terrible and totally undermined.

Bob: We treat our children and our friends a lot better than we treat ourselves in this process. The answer is to find a more positive, kinder, gentler, more affirming approach.

Having read this dialogue, is there a message for you?

ASK YOURSELF

Do I place undue pressure on myself?
What lessons could I learn about how to treat myself more kindly?

We hope that this chapter has given you a lot of ideas and information about what to do when you feel unmotivated. As you can see, the Test Team also went through low periods but, like them, there is no reason you have to stay unmotivated if you do not wish to.

13

GROWing further

Renewing your achievement
Continuing with GROW by yourself or with others
Our future vision

So how did you do? Naturally we hope you have had a lot of success from your experience of working through this book and the GROW process. However, we recognise that each individual will have had a different experience.

Reviewing your achievement

Now is a good time to review what you achieved from reading this book and using the GROW process. Which of the following outcomes did you have?

Achieved complete success

Perhaps you found the GROW process easy and natural to work with and experienced some great wins? If so, congratulations! We know that achieving a Goal, even with the aid of the

GROW process, takes a lot of time and effort. We do hope you included a way of celebrating your success in your Way Forward and that you fully acknowledged yourself for your achievement.

Some teams just celebrate their success. But Clive Woodward, the coach of the English rugby team who won the World Cup in 2003, reputedly always gets his players together after winning a game to talk about *how* they achieved their success. Here are some questions aimed at discovering what you learned from achieving your Goal.

ASK YOURSELF

Would I have achieved my Goal without the GROW process?

What specifically did the GROW process add?

What insights have been most important for me?

What would I do differently when pursuing another Goal?

Why not go for another Goal right now, or possibly continue to develop the next stage of the one you achieved working through this book? Many participants in the Test Team gained significant personal insights while working through this material. If you have learned something important about yourself you can take this 'gift' and go on to achieve even greater things in your life.

We hope that the GROW process will become a tool which you will use again and again to create change for yourself and possibly assist others to make positive changes in their own lives.

Achieved some success

Perhaps you saw the potential for GROW and made some progress, but not as much as you would have liked? Here are some questions to help you review your experiences and maybe try the GROW process again.

ASK YOURSELF

Did I get stuck with the process or did I simply lose interest?

If I got stuck, where in the process did this happen?

What can I learn about myself from using the GROW process?

If I lost interest, what got in the way and how could I avoid this happening again?

Was my Goal too ambitious?

Could I start again and use the GROW process with a less demanding Goal?

Did I seek out all the support I really needed?

If I didn't, what prevented me from doing this?

What would I do differently if I started the GROW process again?

Few of us have time to spare and achieving a specific Goal usually takes up several hours a week or more. When members of the Test Team lost interest it was invariably because other things got in the way. Consider going back to Chapter 4 – 'Preparing the Ground' – to see if you can create better conditions for working on your Goal. It is possible you will have to give something up to make the space and time to achieve a significant objective.

We really hope that after reviewing your experience with this book you will return to the GROW process and achieve your original Goal or maybe pick another.

Achieved little or no success

Perhaps you liked the idea of achieving a Goal using the GROW process, but somehow you did not really get started? Maybe the process was not right for you, the Goal was not one which really got you motivated, or other things got in the way.

If you can spare a little more time, try answering the following questions.

ASK YOURSELF

How did I approach this book?
Was my approach in any way casual?
How much did I really want to achieve my Goal?
Would my chances of success be increased if I chose a different Goal?
How have I made other changes in the past?
What can I learn from this?

A possible Way Forward could be to look at just one aspect of the GROW process and see what insights there are for you. Take Obstacles, for example. If you can understand better how you deal with them then maybe you could use that knowledge to pick up this book again.

It is also worth looking at how well you set up support structures and used other people to encourage you while achieving your Goal. Maybe you skipped this part altogether? We are convinced that this is an essential element of Goal achievement for most people. You could start with discussing whatever experience you had with this book with someone whose opinion you value and see if you can start again, perhaps gaining their interest and support.

Let us know

Now you have reviewed your progress, why not tell us about it? Feedback from you, the reader, is very important for us as we are very keen to know how well this book has worked for you. Tell us about the insights you have gained, the successes you have achieved, and any frustrations or concerns. We also welcome your suggestions and ideas for making the GROW process even more effective and particularly how to stay motivated as you move towards your goal. Our contact details are:

Bob
email: info@bobgriffiths.com
telephone: 0845 226 3312

Chris
email: info@chriskaday.com
telephone: 0845 226 9464

We look forward to hearing from you.

Continuing with GROW by yourself or with others

If you have achieved your Goal, you now know how the GROW process works and understand why it is so effective at producing positive results.

There is no limit to what you can achieve next with this deceptively simple process. Maybe you could go for a much larger life Goal or possibly a 'being' Goal which will affect the quality of the relationship you have with yourself and with others. You might like to review Chapter 5 – 'Goal types and topics' – to pick something really challenging and pertinent to you right now.

Not only can you now go on to work on another Goal, but you can also introduce the GROW process to others. Most people are used to hearing about the dreams and frustrations of their friends and acquaintances. You might hear them say 'I'm really bored with my job right now'; 'I couldn't get into my favourite dress last night'; 'I really wish I could find a loving partner'. Having read this book you now know a simple, well documented process that they could use to get what they want.

You could even lend them this book and help them to work through it. Who better to support them than someone who is familiar with the GROW process and has used it to get a definite result?

Perhaps you can use the GROW process with those in your place of work or other group situation. All communities need a common purpose and have tasks to achieve. The GROW process is ideal in these situations.

As we move from the information to the transformation society more and more individuals are setting higher aspirations in terms of personal growth and change. This book represents an important step forward in this respect and we hope you will keep on GROWing.

Our future vision

You don't have to be the proverbial man or woman from Mars to see that the world is full of confusion and lack of clarity. At the same time, virtually everyone has hopes dreams and ambitions, both complex and simple, which they would like to turn into reality.

Writing this book has confirmed our confidence in the GROW process as a clear and effective method for achieving Goals. We feel it is especially relevant in today's hectic world where time is precious and the need to focus on what we want is essential. Our vision is to empower thousands of people to achieve a Goal of their choosing and this book is an important part of this aim.

We are both fully committed to exposing our pioneering work with the GROW process to an even wider audience. To make this happen we are:

- creating more tools and content to take over from where this book has left off, which will be published in a variety of formats.

- carrying out live demonstrations of the GROW process in workshops and events.
- encouraging the building of communities focused on helping others to achieve their Goals using the GROW process.
- building the GROW process into valuable software tools for individuals and groups to make Goal achievement even more efficient and successful.
- providing a referral service for individuals and organisations who wish to work with a 'GROW-trained' coach.

You can find out more about these activities on our individual websites at www.bobgriffiths.com and www.chriskaday.com.

Thank you for committing your time and energy to the GROW process and this book. We look forward to playing a continuing role in helping you to GROW even further.

Appendix 1

Using GROW for shared Goals

Up to this point you have been using GROW to achieve your own Goals by yourself, albeit with support. The same principles can be used when you are working with others. In this section we will show you how to apply GROW to achieve a shared Goal while working with one or more other people.

As we mentioned at the beginning of the book, you might well be considering a joint Goal in association with another person. If it is your life partner then this could be taking an annual vacation, buying a house, improving your relationship in some way, moving to a new area or country, having children, creating college funds, going from a two-income household down to a one-income household, and so on.

Alternatively, if you are working with a group of people on a special project you can use GROW to improve the way you work together. There are many situations where group Goals can be achieved using the GROW process. These could include sporting and social clubs, where you might be planning a successful event, recruiting more members or raising funds.

In the work arena, GROW provides a means for teams to quickly bond and work together effectively. It has been used for a myriad of applications: for instance, as a project planning tool, to increase market share, solve production problems or create new products. In virtually any situation where people have to work together to solve a problem or achieve a Goal, GROW provides a means to do it successfully. Indeed, just by heading up five slides on a PowerPoint presentation or pages on a flip chart with Goal, Reality, Obstacles, Options and Way Forward, you have the skeleton of a process for progressing any issue.

What is the value of using GROW with others?

Most of the exercises and ideas you will find in this book are equally applicable whether you are using GROW by yourself or with others. However, if you are using GROW with more than one person, there are definite advantages as compared to doing it by yourself. A group will have:

1   a common methodology – everyone agrees how the issues will be addressed;
2   a clearly defined end point – the Goal;
3   reduced conflict – if everyone agrees where they are going and how they are going to get there the possibilities for conflict are greatly reduced;
4   the opportunity for individuals to get encouragement, feedback and support from other team members;
5   more opportunity to discover the real Obstacles and develop creative and realistic Options;
6   more resources to carry out the action steps.

As with any human endeavour, there is always the possibility that human factors such as personality clashes or hidden agendas can disrupt progress. While there is no guarantee, here are some simple guidelines that will greatly increase your effectiveness in using GROW within a group:

1 Choose your Goal carefully. It should be an objective which everyone agrees is worthwhile and achievable. If you are facing a particularly complex issue, break it down into sub Goals and use GROW on each sub Goal.

2 Ensure your Goals have the full commitment of all parties. If there is not commitment at the start of the process the Goal is bound to unravel as it progresses.

3 Set clear boundaries around the Goal so it does not creep into other aspects of the business or organisation. Other issues might be thrown up but they can be the subject of separate GROW processes.

4 Decide how often you are going to meet, how long the meetings will last and whether they will be in person, over the telephone or using the Internet.

5 Decide who is going to run the process or if you are going to share the responsibilities equally.

6 Acknowledge progress and the contribution of every individual participant, especially those who give most.

7 Make sure that all views and contributions are accepted and welcomed. Ideally, keep an electronic or paper record of contributions and progress.

8 Have a clear record of who is going to be responsible for which action points and when they will be completed.

9 Arrange some review times to check how you are all doing with the GROW process, as sometimes you can be too close for comfort.

If GROW is not working

GROW will produce positive results in a wide variety of circumstances. If it is not working there could be a number of reasons:

1 the issue is genuinely not solvable or, alternatively, is too simple;
2 the group are not working through the GROW process properly;
3 interpersonal issues are getting in the way of the group using GROW effectively;
4 the group is being restricted in some way in putting forward the most effective solution.

You will find a lot of information on dealing with these issues in Chapter 12, 'Staying motivated'.

If you find that GROW is not working:

1 acknowledge it as soon as possible so that corrective action can be taken;
2 ask the group for their ideas on how to start making progress;
3 bring in an outsider who does not have the group's 'baggage';
4 see what lessons you can learn about how the company is being run.

Particular issues for couples working with GROW

One might conclude that a relationship already carries with it a common agenda, but that does not necessarily happen just because you enter and leave through the same front door. It is quite possible that setting a common agenda in a partnership or marriage can highlight some serious differences. No two people are alike, and it would be unusual if this did not happen. However, if any differences are resolved with love and respect, then the relationship can be significantly strengthened. You might well consider having a trusted person facilitate a GROW process with you both. They would provide the structure and you would provide the content. If you do decide to work without an outside person, here are some guidelines which will enhance your chances of success.

1   Ensure that the Goal that you agree to set is something that you both really want. Don't swap one Goal for another: that is, don't agree to one of your partner's Goals just so that they'll agree to one of yours. That is not in the spirit of mutual Goal-getting, and again it reduces commitment.
2   Do not use GROW if there are significant emotional issues between you which are seriously affecting communication. GROW will only work if there are not too many sub-agendas and individuals are honest with one another. If there are too many 'undercurrents' the process will come to a halt, either in conflict or for reasons no one can apparently explain.
3   Keep building up the sense of partnership between you as you work through the process. If you are honest and respect the other person, progress is much faster.

If you follow the advice in this section while working with others you will stand an excellent chance of achieving out-standing results.

Appendix 2

The history of the GROW process

The GROW process was developed in the UK and used extensively in the corporate coaching market in the late 1980s and 1990s. Many have claimed authorship of GROW as a way of achieving Goals. It is worth noting that Graham Alexander and Sir John Whitmore, both well known in the world of coaching, made significant contributions.

Part of the reason we wrote this book is that while GROW is very well known in the business arena it also has a multitude of applications in everyday life that have not been fully explored. We wanted to make the process more widely known in other fields where individuals would benefit by having an effective, structured methodology to achieve Goals. GROW can be used by anyone, whatever their vocation, age or personal circumstances. While there are many methodologies that can be used to address problems, the value of GROW is that it is easily understood, straightforward to apply and very thorough. In addition, once you have a basic understanding of how it works, it is possible to apply it to an amazing variety of issues in a very effective way.

The GROW principle and the Inner Game

The principle behind the GROW process is rooted in the Inner Game theory developed by Timothy Gallwey, a tennis coach who was frustrated by the limitations of conventional sports coaching methods. He noticed that he could often see the faults in a player's game, but that simply telling him what to do to improve did not bring about lasting change.

For instance, if a player were not keeping his eye on the ball, most coaches would give advice such as: 'Keep your eye on the ball.' When a player received this sort of instruction he would try to do what the coach was asking him and watch the ball more closely. Unfortunately, no one can keep instructions in the front of their minds for long, so players usually slipped back into their old habits and both coaches and players grew increasingly frustrated.

So one day, instead of giving an instruction, Gallwey asked:

'Can you say "bounce" out loud when the ball bounces and "hit" out loud when you hit the ball?'

In order to do this, players had to keep their eyes on the ball but no longer had a voice in their heads repeating the words 'I must keep my eye on the ball.' At this, their play started to improve markedly and the Inner Game method of coaching was born.

From then on, whenever Gallwey wanted a player to change, he no longer gave instructions but would, instead, ask questions that would help the player discover for himself what worked and what needed to change.

The first stage in this process would be to set a target for the player. For instance, in a situation where a player was serving 'out' a lot of the time, Gallwey would ask him how many first serves out of ten he would like to get 'in'. In this way, together, they created a clear **Goal**.

Then he would ask the player to serve ten balls and see how many he got in. In this way he helped the player define his **Reality**.

The next stage might be to ask him to observe what he was doing differently when the serve went 'in' from when it went 'out', thereby helping the player to get in touch with his **Obstacles** and **Options**. By really looking at what was happening, players learnt for themselves what they needed to change in order to meet their serving targets. This gave players a clear **Way Forward**.

In the example using Gallwey and his tennis players, the basic methodology of GROW was present from the start.

A number of principles have been developed out of Gallwey's experience with tennis players. While they originate from sport, the same principles can be applied to many learning situations. For example:

1   It is more effective to focus your attention on a relevant aspect of what is actually happening while you are learning, instead of what you 'should' be doing or trying to get it 'right' according to someone else's perspective. This may seem blindingly obvious; however, in practice it rarely happens. In our tennis example the player would probably be focusing on trying to remember what the last coach said about serving and would then become more and more frustrated if his attempts at improvement did not work.

2   The best learning happens when we are focusing on the present. This means we are not struggling to prove or remember something but rather making discoveries as we go along.

3   We can easily interfere with the learning process by, for instance, trying to look good or using a lot of unfocused effort. The less we interfere with our learning, the faster we progress.

While the Inner Game was developed in sport, the coaches using it realised they could apply the principles in other learning situations. GROW was developed to provide a structured framework to use the principles of the Inner Game to achieve

Goals. The originators saw that, just as in sport, many individuals were struggling to achieve their Goals because they were not learning from experience and were not aware of the knowledge within themselves that would help them.

Just as an Inner Game coach guides you by asking questions in order to learn a sport, the exercises and questions in this book will guide you through the stages of GROW in order to reach your Goal. Each of the stages of the process has been designed to focus your awareness on an important aspect of Goal achievement. We would go as far as saying that if you follow GROW carefully and honestly, get good support and put energy and enthusiasm into your efforts, it is hard *not* to achieve your Goal. Everybody in the Test Team, whether they achieved their Goal or not, commented that they had learned an immense amount from using GROW. You too can have a successful and exciting experience with the process. We wish you the very best.

Appendix 3

Further reading

If you would like to read further about GROW we suggest the following books.

Coaching for Performance,
John Whitmore (2002, 3rd edition, London: Nicholas Brealey)

The Tao of Coaching,
Max Landsberg (2003, London: Profile Books)

Co-active Coaching: New Skills for Coaching People Toward Success in Work and Life, Laura Whitworth, Henry Kimsey-House and Phil Sandahl (1998, Palo Alto, California: Davis-Black)